Sonoma County

Wine Library

THE SUBTLE ALCHEMIST

THE

Subtle Alchemist

A BOOK OF WINE

by George Rainbird
& Ronald Searle

Chateau Whichford

Reserve de G. Rainbird
Appellation Controleé

MICHAEL JOSEPH · LONDON

First published in Great Britain as
THE POCKET BOOK OF WINE
by Evans Brothers Ltd
Revised edition first published by
Michael Joseph Limited, 52 Bedford Square, London WC1
1973

© 1973 by George Rainbird
© in illustrations 1973 by Ronald Searle

ISBN 0 7181 1117 6

Set and printed in Great Britain by
Westerham Press, at Westerham, Kent
in Apollo type, eleven point leaded, and bound
by James Burn at Esher, Surrey

CONTENTS

5

Contents

In memory of my guide, philosopher and friend,
André Simon,
who said it all before and so much better

The Grape that can with Logic absolute
The Two-and-Seventy jarring Sects confute
The subtle Alchemist that in a Trice
Life's leaden Metal into Gold transmute
                                    Omar Khayyám

INTRODUCTION

Wine is the fermented juice of the grape. It is not a concoction made from parsnips, potatoes or dandelions, however good it may be, and no further reference will be made to such cordials in these pages. I make this distinction at once because I believe there to be an ever-expanding public who are interested in making them and I would not want them to be under any illusion about the nature of this book which is about wine, and wine alone; not even spirits are mentioned except, of course, brandy which is a distillation of wine.

Wine may mean many things to many people, from the connoisseur delving in his cellar for his last bottle of Château Lafite '99, to the French peasant reaching for his litre bottle of local, or more likely imported, red wine from the nearest *alimentation*. To the connoisseur, the Lafite '99 will mean a great moment in time when for half an hour or so the true magic may be revealed and he and his privileged friends (for great wine is never drunk alone) will discuss and compare the bouquet and colour, the after-taste and manifold merits of this incomparable wine; they will shake their heads slowly after the last drops in their glasses have been drunk and will give thanks to God for having been privileged to be present, and hope devoutly that they will be spared to share such another miracle.

To the peasant, wine is life itself, just as important as his daily bread and more important than almost anything else. The wine he drinks, as like as not, will come from the Midi, a large area under the Pyrénées stretching roughly between

Carcassonne and Avignon, and making an enormous quantity of dull, fruity wine, often assisted with wines from Algeria and possibly Tunisia and Morocco. The drinker will not worry very much about it; he will take it for what it is, one of the more agreeable necessities of life, providing both food and drink and making the world a rather better place to live in. On high days and holidays your peasant may indulge in a bottle of sound Bordeaux or Burgundy according to whether he likes his wine dry or sweet, and he'll be well satisfied thereby. He will probably die without ever drinking the wine of one of the great châteaux of Bordeaux or famous domaines of Burgundy.

Somewhere between the connoisseur and the peasant there lies an enormous class of intelligent human beings who like wine. People who, having tasted wine and having found it good, want to know rather more about it, though not necessarily wanting to join the ranks of those connoisseurs who compare only the greatest and rarest wines which, in any case, are beyond the purses of most of us. Let us assume that we *like* wine, and so long as we have this in common, we can use our intelligence and at least four of the five senses to discriminate and to choose wine which for us will be better than other wines in the same class. One doesn't have to be a wine snob to appreciate good or great wine, but it is a great mistake not to be able to know and appreciate one when you find it. The important thing is to like wine for what it is, to drink only honest wines whether they be cheap or not, and then to enjoy them for what they are and not what they might be.

This book, then, is intended as a guide to what constitutes an honest wine. This is harder to come by than you might think. It is not so easy to define either, for, as will be seen later, a dishonest wine in Bordeaux – that is, a wine to which sugar has been added at the time of fermentation, could be a completely honest wine in Burgundy where it is permitted to *chaptalize* by the addition of sugar, although in strictly controlled quantities. There are good reasons for this.

There is a good deal of truth in the saying that Paris alone consumes twice the annual output of Beaujolais, and if we add the demand for Beaujolais all over the world, it will be seen that the genuine Beaujolais is extremely difficult to come by. This is an example of what I mean by a *dishonest* wine, for in order to meet the world demand for Beaujolais (even if we leave out Paris) the custom is to blend (or 'stretch' as they say in the trade) the true Beaujolais with the wines from, possibly Algeria, Malta, Australia, or any other country providing cheap, sound, red wine. The result is not as bad as it would sound, because the shippers know their job and also know perfectly well that if they don't produce a palatable wine, which is, of course, sold at a rather higher price than ordinary wine, the demand for so-called Beaujolais will decline, and they will be out of business. But nevertheless, there is very little real Beaujolais in most of the Beaujolais sold in this country today, and I suppose it would be not far from the truth to say that comparatively few drinkers of this excellent wine have ever tasted a really genuine one. From this kind of thing the buyer has one sure way of protecting himself; he can buy only Beaujolais which is shipped by a reputable firm and is marked clearly '*Appellation Contrôlée*'. If he does this and he buys only from a wine merchant of strict reputation, he has at least obtained wine from Beaujolais with a good birth certificate, although it can mean no more than that, for as in every other wine, there are good, bad and indifferent Beaujolais of good, bad and indifferent years. There is not much difference in the price, although, of course, there is bound to be some, between that of a reputable and genuine Beaujolais and most of the fake wines bearing that name. The object of this book is to help discerning and intelligent readers to distinguish and discriminate.

One last word – in order to know wine you must drink wine. When you drink wine, use those taste buds with which you are endowed, and, above all, develop curiosity about wine in all its legitimate forms. Make your own classifications and your own rules; learn to know what you like and like what you know. If, for some reason or other, you prefer to drink a white wine with your steak, drink it: if you travel a lot you will know there are a good many places in this world where you can buy only the local wine to drink with whatever you are eating. When in a red wine country, in some parts of Spain, for instance, you would drink red wine with your fish and like it, and the meal will be none the worse for it.

Since this is a book about wine and the enjoyment thereof for plain people, I have avoided pretentious wine jargon and too much technical description; only the most important grapes used in wine making are named. If the reader is tempted to know more, there are plenty of large books about each chapter subject for him to read, which I hope he will, glass in hand and bottle at side.

> *Which cheers the sad, revives the old, inspires*
> *The young, makes weariness forget his toil,*
> *And fear her danger; opens a new world*
> *When this, the present, palls.*
>
> Byron: *Sardanapalus*

1. ON WINE IN GENERAL

Wine, as we have said, is the fermented juice of the grape and it is made and has been made since the beginning of recorded time in all the countries of the world where grapes are grown. The vine thrives in all kinds of climate and on all types of soil, except in the frozen North, and in equatorial regions. The vine will grow where little else will thrive. This is true also of the olive, and between them the vine and the olive tree can and do provide most that is necessary to keep man healthy and wealthy and wise.

In AD 92 the Emperor Domitian ordered that a large part of the wine-growing areas in Gaul should be denuded of their vines in order to plant wheat to fill the granaries of

Rome, and this order was duly carried out. But in Champagne, where the soil is thin on the chalk hills of the Valley of the Marne, even wheat would not grow, and he lost his labour and the Gauls lost their wine – a very poor bargain for both parties.

Italy at that time (or at any time since) had no need of wine from abroad; it grew the vine prosperously everywhere, and the making of wine had reached far greater refinement and development centuries before the French made full use of their natural resources in the making of fine wine. Even before Rome, in the days of classical Greece, wine was made and venerated according to its district and the vintner, and the symbols of the vine, its grapes and leaves, and its protecting deity, Bacchus, all decorate profusely the famous and beautiful attic *kraters* and pottery cups of the period.

Wine has been found and depicted in wall paintings in the earliest Egyptian tombs. The most reliable proofs of the length of the reign of Pharaoh Tutankhamen are the winejars found intact (with rather 'corked' wine still inside!) bearing the seal of the Royal Vineyards and stamped with an inscription to the effect that the wines were made in the ninth year of the Pharaoh's reign. He died about 1350 BC, long before the Israelites under Moses left Egypt.

Three things go into the making of wine, whether it be good, bad or indifferent. Firstly, the soil from which the vine grows, secondly, the sun or the amount of sunshine which shines upon the vine in any given year and, thirdly, the hand of the *vigneron* who makes the wine. The first is immovable and permanent, the second variable and the third and last is human. When these three come into alignment, the result can be a near miracle, and by the grace of God this sometimes happens.

Obviously, the first element, the soil upon which the vines are grown, does not alter from year to year, but like any other soil it can become exhausted if it is not constantly fed with the right kind of humus, although its mineral-bearing qualities will be unimpaired whatever happens. And it is just these mineral-bearing qualities which provide those mysterious saccharomyces and yeasts which form in the bloom of the grape and which, in conjunction with the fermenting elements, in the sugar of the grape itself, form the special flavour and character of the grape.

It is unquestionably true that the grapes from which the finest wines are made grow on the thinnest of soils, and consequently those with the smallest of yields, and from which it must follow that the wine made therefrom is in the smallest quantity. The quality of the soil can change from field to field, and one only has to travel through the English countryside by car or train in the early spring when the fields are fresh-harrowed, to see the change in the soil, especially on a chalky country. One-half of the field may be quite white and then suddenly the whole colour value changes and the other end is brown. So it is with many vineyards, and it is quite possible and, indeed, true that only a narrow path will separate the vineyard making the wine of the very first order from another producing grapes which are of the third or fourth growth. This is the first element in wine-making; the soil upon which the grapes are grown, which, in their turn, will be vulnerable to sun and storm, and which must be kept in first-class condition by the man who makes the wine.

The second factor is the sun itself and is, of course, responsible for most of the worries of the vineyard. By sun, I also mean the lack of it, for generally speaking, it can be assumed that if the grapes ripen, you will get good wine, and if they do not ripen properly, you won't. But there are varying degrees of ripeness, and it is this factor which makes all the difference to a good, bad or indifferent year.

If the sun shines when the buds are burgeoning on the vine, it is a very good thing; and if the sun shines when the flowers are blooming, that is also a good thing, but most of all the sun is wanted when the grapes have formed and are beginning to swell. Then a little rain won't hurt, and if a fine month is experienced before the vintage, you are likely to get some extraordinarily good wine. If, on the other hand, the weather is wet and damp, all the very horrible diseases which the vine grower has to contend with will start to raise their extremely ugly heads – nasty things connected with mildew and bugs which thrive in damp and wet and all take their toll to reduce the crop, and not only that, to spoil the wine. For the function of the sun is to promote the sugar in the grape which becomes alcohol in fermentation.

Too much sun, on the other hand, will also do damage, although not by any means on the same scale. The grapes become *brulé*, or burnt, and the wine is hot and rather harsh, and it is for this reason that some of the Greek and Mediterranean wine is pretty harsh stuff.

By and large, it can be taken as a fairly competent guide to assume that there can be no good wine of a bad year, although it is quite possible to have a bad wine of a good year. The wine merchant, or shall we say *some* wine merchants, will not subscribe to this for fairly obvious reasons, but I defy anybody to give me a *good* honest wine of 1902 or 1903 or, to be nearer, 1930, 1931 or 1932, and nearer still, 1951 or 1954. There may be good wines in these years, but I have never seen one. This does not, however, mean that the wine is necessarily undrinkable, because here the *vigneron* will sometimes, if he is allowed to, as he is in Burgundy and most

19

parts of France, bring art to the aid of nature, and by the judicious and extremely skilful addition of a little sugar, can put into the wine what the sun and weather have failed to provide for it. The result is not a true wine, or even by any manner of means, to be termed fine, or great wine, but it is certainly palatable. A good example of this is 1951 where the weather was so bad in the Bordeaux district that a special regulation was made to allow the growers to *chaptalize* or sugar the wine, a method which is under normal circumstances proscribed by law in the Bordeaux area. The resulting wine isn't by any means unpalatable, but it is distinctly odd and, as a friend of mine remarked on being given a bottle of a first growth 1951 : 'As Bordeaux, this is an extraordinarily good Burgundy.' The great years, however, have been uniformly sunny with just enough rain to put heart into the berries. Such a year was 1929, and probably the finest wines that I have ever drunk have been '29s; '47 and '53 were rather similar.

But even now the '53s are showing some signs of 'going over the hill' and while still very splendid if you have any in your cellars you should drink it soon. The best wine I ever drank was a Château Margaux 1870 in its 91st year and which truly deserved to be drunk on one's knees, but this was an exceptional wine and was very hard when it was made: hence its longevity. I also had some superb 1899–1900s but I assumed these are now all long drunk and not within the compass of any person who is likely to read this book. But if by any chance the reader should be able to get hold of a bottle of Cheval Blanc 1947 bottled at the château he will be in the presence of true greatness – possibly the finest wine made in a century.

We have now dealt with the soil, which is permanent, and the sun, which is extremely variable, and assuming that we have the soil and we get fine sun, we can agree that we shall have some very good wine provided that it is well made.

The basic process of making wine is simple and universal. The grapes are gathered; they are stripped (in most places) of their stalks, and they are dumped together in a large press and pressed; the juice is run off into large vats, and in a few hours fermentation commences. (If red wine is being made, the black grape skins are left in, for it is the pigment in the grape skins dissolved in fermentation which gives red wine its colour. White wine is often made from black grapes, cf. Champagne, but the skins are removed before fermentation starts.) This fermentation is, as it is called, boisterous; that is, it bubbles away rather like a mud volcano. At just the right time, the *vigneron* will stop the first fermentation by drawing off the wine into barrels and a period of secondary fermentation is commenced. This varies from place to place and according to the method of storage, but let us assume that we are discussing very good wine in, say, the Bordeaux district. In the first year, the wine is stored in *barriques* – that is, large barrels containing about a hogshead (or 48 gallons) in what is called the *chais* which is the large hall or shed adjoining the *pressoir* where the wine is made and where the fermenting vats stand, usually above ground, and where the new wine is racked by transferring it from barrel to barrel, about three times during the first year, while undergoing its slow secondary fermentation. From the *chais* the wine is removed to the cellar where it is racked yet again, once in its second year, and in the third year it is bottled. In the case of minor wines, and more common wines (perhaps 'little wines' is a better expression), the second fermentation is accelerated by technical processes as it is intended for quick consumption – it is not expected to adorn your cellar or mine for ten or twenty years before it is drunk.

But to return to our better wines – in the third year it is bottled. In all these conditions, there is a very human factor – that of timing. In the moment of time when God ordains that a wine should be at its most perfect best, the vintner must first of all stop fermentation in the vat by putting his wine into barrels; he must choose the exact (and by exact, I don't mean to the minute, but certainly within a few days) time in which the wine in its first year should be racked, and again in the second year, and above all, the moment in time when the wine in the barrel shall be bottled.

The vast majority of wine is exported in bulk – that is to say, the barrel is sent to England or wherever it may be, after the secondary fermentations have stopped, and before bottling. Obviously, it is much cheaper and easier to move wine in quantities of 50 gallons than in a case of a dozen bottles – 2 gallons – and at this stage, I must tell you about the necessity of using a wine merchant of reputation. If the wine is bottled at its château or domaine or schloss, it is to be assumed that the *vigneron* will know the best moment at which to bottle his own wine. If he is a bad *vigneron*, he won't. That is why many wines have ceased to live up to their reputations. It is much the same with your wine merchant who imports his wine in barrels – he must by constant tasting and by good cellarage choose the day on which that wine should be bottled in order to give it its very best chance. This is a matter of great experience and not a little inspiration.

Our wine is now in the bottles and we must assume that whether it is done in the château or whether it is done in the cellars of a local and trusted wine merchant, or in the bonded store in London, that the expert has done his job properly and the wine has been given its best chance on the day of bottling.

Now there is the little matter of the cork, and it is upon the cork that the whole reputation of the wine will rest from the time of bottling forward, for wine is rendered bad only through the air which obviously cannot reach the wine through the bottle and therefore must come through the cork. If you buy your wine château-bottled or if you buy it through a first-class wine merchant, you will find they are using what is called the long cork (which is $2\frac{1}{4}$ inches long) even on moderate qualities of wine. Wine merchants who wish to save money (and indeed if the wine is to be drunk very quickly after bottling there can be nothing wrong in this) use a short and, therefore, cheaper cork. The better the cork the better you can keep your wine, because the air will not get through it quite so quickly. Cheap corks are short and porous and the air will get in and will turn your wine into vinegar.

Nowadays one sees all kinds of corks for cheap wine – plastic (ugh!), even crown corks for *ordinaires* in France, and I don't doubt they do their job for wine intended for consumption within a few days.

These are the many factors natural and human which militate against the production of the truly great bottle of wine and so it must be, but you and I are not wine snobs. If we come across a really great bottle of wine we shall drink it on bended knees (metaphorically at least), but we will also take our pleasure when we can and be satisfied with a good deal less, and by satisfied, I mean extremely happy, too. As I write these words, I have at my elbow an excellent glass of dry Portuguese white wine; it costs but very little. It is clean, it is honest and I am very happy with it.

2. ON THE SERVICE OF WINE

People who do not trouble to serve wine properly in their own homes hardly deserve to drink it, because there is all the difference in the world between wine which is brought to the table at its best and wine which is merely poured out of a bottle without thought to its condition. Let us take the wine in our cellar, if we have one, or in the cupboard where we keep our wines if we have not.

Wine is best kept at a temperature of 55° F but won't hurt very much if your cellar (or cupboard) goes down a few degrees in winter or goes up to 60° in summer. Temperatures must, however, be kept reasonably constant and if you freeze your wine in winter and boil it in summer, you can hardly expect to get much more than an intoxicating liquid out of your bottle, or perhaps only vinegar. If you can control your cellar, there should be ventilation of some sort, but no great harm will be done to the wine if there is not, as may be proved by the well-authenticated stories of fathers who traditionally wall up a specially stocked cellar of wine on the birth of their first-born son, to be opened after he comes of age, or later. In some places, like Limberg in South Holland, this kind of thing has been going on for some hundreds of years, so we may take it that if ventilation had much to do with the keeping quality of wine, the practice would have stopped a long while ago.

The next point to remember is that wine must always lie on its side and the reason for this is twofold: firstly, that the wine shall cover the cork and thus help to seal itself from air entering through the cork (for obviously, if there were a space between the cork and the wine, this would certainly be a breeding ground for the kind of microbe that will start the trouble in the wine), and, secondly, to allow any sediment or 'crust' to settle in the bottom of the bottle while it is resting. There have been many tragic tales on this subject; the one that comes readily to mind is that of a spiteful aunt who, having to leave her cellar and her property to a particularly disliked nephew, arranged for all the bottles of wine to be stood up and all the bottles of spirit to be laid on their sides, with the net result that when the nephew inherited, both were worthless. If a bottle of wine is left in a standing position for a long period, the cork will shrink, and then that is the end of the wine.

The best way to store your wine is in bins, if you have a cellar, or in the simple wire racks which may be bought from people like Fortnum & Mason or Robert Jackson in Piccadilly, at so much per hole. They can be made in any size to fit whatever space you have available, and if you like they can go up in steps to fit in a cupboard under stairs.

With your wine in reasonable condition, it can be served, and this is the moment which the wine-lover has long awaited.

White wines can be taken direct to the table, and, according to the temperature of your cellar, may be served at any time, provided they are cold. Some friends of mine, and I do myself, keep the light beverage wines like Entre Deux Mers or Bordeaux or the dry white Portuguese wine I mentioned or white wines from Spain in the refrigerator, so that they can be taken out at any time and are always very cold, as indeed they should be. On the other hand, it is a very great mistake to serve really fine white wine like white Burgundy from Meursault or Montrachet, or the fine German Hocks and Moselles, or indeed any of the finer white wines quite so cold as this. They need to be chilled and not frozen, and are quite all right if served straight from the cellar provided the temperature is not more than 50–55°, plus a little extra cold which can be provided by no more, say, than a quarter or half an hour in the refrigerator. This is also true of Champagne, which is at its very best when really cold, but not frozen.

Rosé wines which are always uniformly light beverage wines (there are one or two exceptions) should be served really cold, and indeed, to my taste, are not really palatable otherwise; even important rosé wines, like those from Tavel near Avignon in the Rhône Valley, are best served very cold.

There are very few red wines, however, which derive any benefit from being chilled (the red wine of Provence is an exception), and, in general, the best way to serve them is at room temperature. Another possible exception to this rule is Beaujolais : there is an informed school of thought which thinks that Beaujolais should be drunk very cold. Certainly it tastes delicious either way. It must be remembered, however, that good red wine can be spoiled by being too warm and I have far too many recollections of being honoured by my host with a superb bottle of claret served, it seemed to me, just off the boil, and completely ruined. It is much better to serve red wine too cold, than too hot, but there is really no reason for either, especially in your own home. My general practice, and I can recommend it to you, is to decant red wine for luncheon after breakfast, and red wine for dinner any time after five or six o'clock. Leave the decanter or the bottle open in your dining-room, or, better still, put it with the saucepans on the rack in the kitchen for a couple of hours, and it should be about right. Never, never, never, repeat never, plunge the bottle or the decanter into hot water – it merely warms the outside of the wine and causes all sorts of circulations to be set up, and does the wine no good at all. I prefer to decant all my red wine, whether it be cheap, medium or dear. I personally think wine looks better in a decanter, and it will certainly give the wine a chance to breathe before drinking. On this matter of decanting, it is necessary to use intelligence and sometimes care, but it is always simple.

For your beverage wines – that is to say, those wines which you will probably drink as a matter of course with some or all of your meals – it is not necessary to go through the ritual of decanting over a candle. Use a decanter which is perfectly clear and white, i.e. colourless (they can be purchased quite cheaply in almost any junk shop), and pour your wine in just as though you were pouring it into a glass. That is all you need do. With the better clarets, some Burgundies and port, especially vintage port, you have to be more careful, but again, it is always a simple, and rather a pleasant ritual. You will need for this operation a cradle, just the usual wicker cradle which can be bought from almost any store, and which you see commonly and quite unnecessarily used in most restaurants. Take the cradle to the bin; take out your bottle from the bin and place it in the cradle in the same position in which it is lying in the bin, that is, with the sediment still in the bottom of the bottle. Take your cradle to the table and remove the cork carefully after wiping the top of the bottle, both before and after the removal of the cork, and the neck and shoulders of the bottle. Grasp the bottom of the bottle with your right hand and remove it from the cradle and hold it over a lighted candle so that you can see the flame of the candle through the wine at the point where the neck joins the shoulder of the bottle. Decant the wine steadily in one pour, not letting the wine regurgitate back into the bottle by altering the position of the bottle above horizontal. Observe, meanwhile, the flame of the candle through the red wine, and as the bottle empties you will immediately perceive the crust at the bottom of the bottle starting to come through the neck. It does not matter about an odd wisp or two, but when the main body of the crust starts to move through the neck stop pouring immediately and either use the rest of the wine for cooking or throw it away. Even though there may be a quarter of a bottle left, it is of no earthly use and you will only spoil what you have already decanted by continuing to pour. When this operation is finished, you should have a candle-bright crimson wine in your decanter, which should be a delight to see and a greater delight to drink.

Port is, however, a special subject, especially if it is one of the older vintages, and you may have considerable trouble in getting out your cork in one piece, because this type of wine

tends to rot the cork and that is why many of the older ports have been recorked. If the cork breaks, then I advise you to get an ordinary glass jug and a very fine tea or coffee strainer, put the strainer on top of the glass jug and continue as though you were pouring into the decanter, after you have fished out the pieces of broken cork as best you can. You will also find in the port itself a substance known as 'beeswing', which is not in itself as harmful to the wine as the very much heavier crust at the bottom of the bottle, and of course, if you are using a strainer, the beeswing will be caught in it, but if you are not and are decanting straight from bottle to decanter, it will do no great harm if a few pieces of beeswing get in. Both beeswing and crust are formed from living organisms in the wine and seem to have an essential part in the development of this superb and rather now out-dated wine we call port. In my opinion, port is about the most difficult wine to decant properly and most worth the trouble. I keep in my cellar a pair of bottle tongs for really special bottles (or I did when I had any special bottles, but, alas, they have long since gone). For my last bottle of Sandeman's Jubilee 1887, for instance, I nipped off the top of the bottle complete with the tongs – it is quite a simple operation. The tongs, which are of the right size for the neck of a port bottle, are heated until they are nearly white-hot, put round the neck of the bottle for a few seconds and then a wet rag is wrapped round the top and the neck snaps off quite cleanly without disturbing the cork, which would almost certainly be bad.

From my experience, the only wines that need to be dealt with by the kind of careful decanting which I have described are clarets over five years old, and these of course include all the red wines of Bordeaux such as St Emilion, Pomerol, the red districts of Graves and, most importantly, the Médoc.

Some old Burgundies need the same treatment, and almost all the classic Burgundies from the Côte des Nuits and the Côte d'Or (but only if they are a few years old); crusted or vintage ports certainly, but I can't really think of any other red wine that needs special treatment. Most of the little red wines of France, including the famous Beaujolais, nearly all English-bottled Burgundies; all the wines of Anjou and the Loire, the Rhône wines, throw hardly any sediment and need not be fussed with. If in doubt, wipe the bottle and hold it over a candle and you can see for yourself.

The affectation of most restaurants in bringing wine to the table carefully nursed in the cradle is, in most cases, pure undiluted nonsense. The first-class *restaurateur* will decant the wine if it needs it and bring it to the table, or put the bottle on the table just as it is, standing upright, which is all that is necessary. There is a very good piece on this in George Orwell's *Down and Out in London and Paris* where he describes how, while working in a Paris restaurant, the wines would be taken from the bin, thrown from hand to hand until they finally reached the dispense bar and would then be brought to the table in a cradle with a napkin round the neck with all the pomp and ceremony imaginable. This, I think, is what usually happens, judging from the condition of the wine when it reaches the table, although, of course, most of them are quite clear because there never was any sediment to get disturbed anyway.

It goes without saying that wine requiring ritual decanting must be rested before the bottle is opened and the time will vary enormously. Of course, cool white wines and most of the minor wines can come straight from your wine cellar and they won't hurt, but fine claret, Burgundy and port can require to rest in the bin for at least three or four weeks from its coming into your cellar and vintage port for three months.

31

Vintage port does not like to be moved at all and it was not for nothing that the wine-loving vicar refused a bishopric because he could not again contemplate moving his port! No great harm is done by standing up the bottle from the bin anything up to a week before it is decanted, in which case, of course, the loose sediment settles on the bottom and you don't put the bottle into a cradle, otherwise the procedure is the same, although I do not think this works out very well with a vintage port. Certainly, it is a method that I use myself sometimes with clarets and domaine-bottled Burgundies.

Madeira and Marsala, although having many affinities with port, for they are made and matured in much the same way, do not normally need very special treatment, as they form little or no crust. I have myself drunk eighteenth-century Madeira which certainly showed no sign of crust, and although they are generally made on the *solera* system (see sherry section, page 131), they do not throw crust even when they are vintage wines made in a certain year.

Sherry is, of course, usually entirely free from crust, but I have drunk some very, very old sherry which proves (for I still have some) almost impossible to decant because its loose sediment has the consistency of mist, and the mere taking of the bottle from the bin, even though the greatest care is used, has sufficed to cloud the wine.

With these wines the rule is for Madeira and Marsala to be served at room temperature, but sherry, apart from the old Amontillados and Olorosas, should be served chilled, especially the *finos*, which are at their very best when slightly iced – but not with ice *inside* the glass!

Brandy is another thing again; in some restaurants, it is considered the thing to heat the brandy glasses on a little spirit stove before pouring the brandy in and handing it to the customer. This is a very great sin and should not be tolerated. Nearly always, the brandy is at room temperature anyway, but it should be served in small glasses and held in the palm of the hand and warmed, if warming be needed, naturally. Nothing really good is to be said of the huge *ballon* glasses which again are sheer affectation, and leave most of the liquid round the glass anyway.

Finally, use a sense of proportion in this matter of the service of wine. All good things, great or small, are worth a little trouble, but to take too much trouble, that is to take everything to the fraction of a degree with younger and cheaper wines, is mere silliness. You will have nothing to complain about if you serve your white and rosé wines quite cold, and your red wines at room temperature. Great wines deserve respect and your special attention, and indeed, if they don't get it, you will only have yourself to blame if the wine is cloudy and dull, for the greater the wine, the more delicate it is and the more easily ruined by bad serving.

3. THE GREAT WINES
OF FRANCE

France is synonymous with wine, and in only seven of the eighty-nine French departments are vines for wine-making not grown. France is by far the largest wine-producing unit in the world, and is responsible, without any doubt whatsoever, for the greatest wines, and also without doubt for some extremely poor wine and, I am sorry to say, some very adulterated wine. But the performance is simply amazing, especially in view of the catastrophic disease cycles which have hit the French vineyards in the last hundred years or so. First of all, it was the oidium which, in 1854, reduced the production of wine to a little more than one-eighth of the average wine production in France. After oidium came the phylloxera, a tiny spider-like bug which attacked the roots of the vines and devastated all the vineyards in France, although there were until recently one or two tiny *enclaves* with pre-phylloxera vines. After phylloxera came the mildew in 1910 which again wrecked French production for a year or two. But the Frenchman has always managed to find the antidote to these diseases, and while he has undoubtedly suffered, most of the vineyards today are healthier than they have ever been. It is, of course, fashionable among my older friends to say that wines have never been the same since phylloxera hit the vineyards of France, but like most of my contemporaries, I have had very little opportunity of tasting pre-phylloxera wines – that is, wines made before about 1890. I have indeed tasted some excellent wine which was certainly pre-phylloxera, but I have also

The Wine Districts of FRANCE

■ Wine Areas
.... International Boundaries

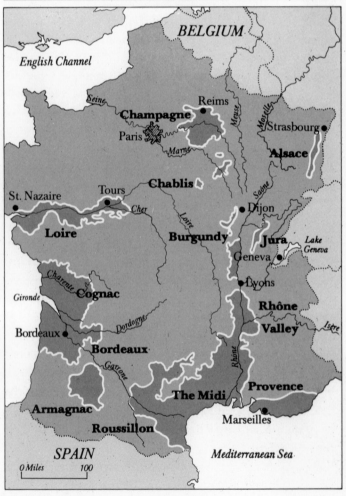

BELGIUM

English Channel

Seine

Champagne

Reims

Paris

Marne

Meuse

Moselle

Strasbourg

Alsace

Chablis

St. Nazaire

Tours

Cher

Loire

Saône

Dijon

Loire

Burgundy

Jura

Lake Geneva

Geneva

Charente

Cognac

Gironde

Dordogne

Lyons

Bordeaux

Bordeaux

Garonne

Rhône Valley

Isère

Rhône

Provence

Armagnac

The Midi

Marseilles

Roussillon

SPAIN

Mediterranean Sea

0 Miles   100

tasted some which, while being post-phylloxera, seemed to me to have such pure magic that I cannot conceive that any wine could be better. Be that as it may, the phylloxera was beaten by the Americans who started the whole thing in the first place, for the phylloxera bug was imported into France in the roots of some experimental American hardy stocks which were immune. Once these stocks were planted in France, the bug quickly transferred its attentions to the native stocks, which were not immune, and spread its ravages through France with the wind. Finally, it was stopped by the wholesale importation of immune American stocks into France on which were grafted the old French vines. France today is therefore one large vineyard of American stock.

Such is the importance of wine to the general economy in France and to the whole well-being of the nation, that the strongest controls are exercised by the Government and by the wine-growers' associations to maintain those pure standards upon which the French reputation has been built but which, by reason of the great demand, have been in the past subjected to all sorts of adulteration and misdescription. All the wine-growing districts and sub-districts of France are now what is called *Appellation Contrôlée* and strict standards are set out on the quality of wine which must be made to certain specifications and be up to certain degrees of alcoholic strength and made within the very clearly set out limits of the district. This ensures that wine sent out with the certificate of *Appellation Contrôlée* has come from the district from which it purports to start, and is composed of the wine of that district and from none other. At least, it starts that way.

The main wine-growing districts of France are as follows: Bordeaux, Burgundy, the Loire, the Rhône Valley, the Midi,

Alsace, the Jura and Savoie, and, last but not least, Champagne. They all have their special characteristics and their special virtues. Good wine is made in all, fine wine in some and great wine in three only. They can be bought, these wines, for very little money – for the young wines of less importance, to quite a lot of money for a first growth Bordeaux of a good year. Writing in 1971 there has recently been a sale of a jeroboam of Château Mouton Rothschild 1929 for the ridiculous sum of £2,860. To pay prices like this merely shows complete lack of all sense and proportion – although it was indeed a very great wine. We shall, however, drink well by choosing carefully the lesser growths of the right years for which we need not pay more than we can afford.

Let us now consider the wines of France, starting with:

BORDEAUX

The red wine of the Bordeaux district is in general called claret, whereas the white wines can be Graves, Barsac, Sauternes, Entre Deux Mers, and so on. Bordeaux was, from the twelfth to the fifteenth centuries, part of the English Crown and it is generally considered that claret derives its name from one of the Earls of Clare who held fief under Henry II of England and his successors. There are many of these English names still active in the Bordeaux district as, for instance, Talbot, whose name still lives in the wine of Château Talbot, one of the best wines of the Médoc. The original Talbot was killed at the battle of Castillon in 1453, which lost Bordeaux and Aquitaine to the English Crown. Before it was known as claret, the wine was known as Gascon wine and it was extremely popular in England during the Middle Ages, if for no other reason than that it was a royal monopoly, and the King had given it to the City of

Bordeaux; consequently there was hardly any competition.

The principal wine-growing districts of Bordeaux are as follows:

The Médoc
Graves
St Emilion and Pomerol
Fronsac
Cérons }
Barsac }
Sauternes }
Sainte-Croix-du-Mont
Côtes de Blaye }
Côtes de Bourg }
Entre Deux Mers
Premières Côtes de Bordeaux

The finest red wines in Bordeaux, and therefore in the world, come from the Médoc, which is on the left bank of the Gironde between Bordeaux and the sea, and from St Emilion, Pomerol and Graves, all of which make red wine of quality. Red wines of second, but still good quality, are made in Côte de Blaye and the Bourgeais, whereas all the other districts make mostly white wines with the exception of Graves, which makes a good deal of fine red wine.

The best dry white wine is made in Graves and the finest sweet white wine is made in the world famous Château d'Yquem in Sauternes. The clean and cheap white wine of Entre Deux Mers which literally means 'between two seas' but is, in fact, between the Garonne and the Dordogne, is made in great quantities and is refreshing and only slightly sweet.

The good red wines of the Côtes de Blaye and Bourgeais

are thoroughly satisfactory, inexpensive, full bodied and have that kiss which signifies the true Bordeaux: a faint touch of sharpness which one finds in all wines of the district, more or less pronounced, according to the quality of the wine and the amount of the sun in that particular year. The wines of Pomerol and St Emilion (with which we shall include Fronsac) are rather richer, fruitier wines than Médoc, and here are made some very important wines indeed.

The red and white wines of Graves have the reputation, and deservedly so, of being by nature fine, well-bred wines. They are not so robust as St Emilion wines and they have not the suave dignity of the great Médocs. One of their number, Château Haut-Brion, is named as one of the four first great growths of Bordeaux, and most of the wines are fully up to Médoc standard, but have perhaps greater *finesse*. They have the reputation of being very good keepers and of outliving the wines of the Médoc, but this I would very much doubt. The soil is poor and stony, hence the name Graves, or gravel, and the output is singularly small, and that is why, with the rising cost of production, many vineyards in Graves have gone out of cultivation or have ceased to cultivate the whole of their acreage.

There are three main types of wine made in the Bordeaux area and this applies, to some extent, to both red and white wines, but principally red. First of all, we have the very finest wine, which is made from the grapes grown on the low hills above the Gironde for the Médoc, and the Dordogne for St Emilion and Pomerol. Those of the Médoc can hardly claim to be called hills – they are gentle slopes and not all that much above the river level, but they were once upon a time under water and the result is a combination of gritty sand and pebbles, which although they can hardly grow anything but vines, have within them those salts and mineral substances which give the wine its delicacy and its tremendous staying power. Then there is a second type of wine which is that made from vast vine-growing areas around Bordeaux like Bourg and Blaye and Entre Deux Mers, which is just good, very good, vine-growing land, slightly better soil and higher yield, but the wine is not great. Thirdly, there is the wine made from what is called the *palus*, which is the richest land of all and actually along the banks of the great rivers. Good wines are made from the *palus*, but they can never be great, although some of them, like the Château de Terrefort in the Gironde, make a very drinkable wine indeed.

Château Bottling

It is necessary to say something at this point on château bottling which is so much a feature of the best Bordeaux vineyards. Château bottling simply means that the wine is actually bottled at the château where the grapes are grown and where the wine is made and matured, and it should therefore represent the wine of that château at its very best, always provided the *vigneron* knows his job. Usually we are safe in assuming that he does, but sometimes not, and consequently, château bottling can never be more than a birth certificate in that you know that it has come from a certain place and is the wine of a certain year bottled at the time the *Maître de Chai* judged it to be at its best. Château-bottled wines are always corked with corks stamped with the name of the château, sometimes with the owner's name and always the date. There have been in the past several châteaux which have not granted château bottling – that is to say, they have never sold the wine bottled at the château, but merely kept what they wanted for their own consumption, and the remainder has been sold in bulk to reputable shippers and wine merchants who bottled the wine. Château Pontet-

Canet is one of these châteaux and Beychevelle another, but both are now granting château bottling, although Pontet-Canet only for the last few years. In the case of wine being sold through a monopoly (for instance Pontet-Canet is owned by the firm of Cruse and therefore, obviously, all the wine of Pontet-Canet will go through their hands), the monopoly will sometimes brand the corks with the name of the château and date, although the wine is in fact bottled in Bordeaux, and this is in some measure an added security to the buyer. This is called *étampé* and the wine may be, and quite probably is, just as good as the château bottled. Apart from these two classes, wines bottled in France need be no better than wines bottled by a first-class wine merchant, but they are more expensive because of the heavier carriage charges and it is only fair to say that bulk wine does not always reach its destination in the best possible condition.

The Médoc

We will start our tour of the Bordeaux wine country with the Médoc, which is itself divided into two districts, Médoc and Haut Médoc; in the latter, the southern area, are found all the greatest wines, although fine wines are made in the Médoc or northern part. Médoc must be dealt with in some detail because of its tremendous importance to wine-lovers all over the world and its influence on wine-making everywhere.

Along the west bank of the Gironde right up to the Bay of Biscay there is a stretch of land some forty-odd miles long. It is not very picturesque, though it rises in parts to low hills and there are swamps and arid wasteland between the wine-growing areas. Along this strip are grown the grapes which make the finest wine in the world.

The actual vine-bearing strip varies in width from a few hundred yards to a mile or so and it is not continuous. There are pockets of vine-growing land which start as suddenly as they cease and a mere footpath may divide worthless land from land which will grow the grapes capable of making the very finest wine. Within these pockets too there are grades of soil; all of it is poor, sandy, gritty, stony and hardly seems capable of growing a single blade of grass. Nevertheless, there are minerals in the soil which, in their turn, feed into the saccharomyces which appear on the bloom of the grape that quality which in fermentation develops, flavours and stabilizes the wine. One château is not exactly like another, either physically or in the wine it produces. There are some cases where a few feet only will divide not only wasteland from fine land, but vineyards making the wine classified as first growth from the vineyard making perhaps a fourth or fifth growth, or even a bourgeois or artisan *cru*. There are some hundreds of châteaux, or estates, in the Médoc and Haut Médoc all producing good wine. There are famous names in the Médoc which conjure up among wine-lovers the greatest of their wine experiences, names like St Julien, Pauillac (mother of no fewer than three of the greatest wines), Margaux, Cantenac, St Estèphe, Macau. These communes and others like them form, as it were, the centre of the wine-growing pockets.

Bordeaux wine, because of its 2,000 years of recorded history, its English court monopoly in the Middle Ages and its export potential because of its lasting properties, has always been prosperous, but never more so than in the first half of the nineteenth century, and it was about 1850 that the Chamber of Commerce in Bordeaux decided to classify the great wines of Médoc; in 1855 what was called the *Grands Crus* Classification was made. This was based on the average prices obtained for the wines from the different estates over a period of years on the general principle that

the best wine gets the best price, and by and large this is perfectly true. The pundits therefore divided the wines of the Médoc into *Grands Crus Classés*, containing no fewer than sixty estates, divided into five *crus* or classes; then the *cru exceptionnel* with only a few, the *cru bourgeois supérieure* from which most of the Médoc wines come and the *cru artisan* which are the *ordinaires*. In addition to this, the *palus* form another very large wine-producing unit, but the wines are never of the finest quality.

Of the sixty great châteaux divided into five growths, in the first growth there are but three – Lafite, Latour and Margaux, and then in honesty and decency the Chamber of Commerce had to let in an outsider – Château Haut-Brion from Graves, whose wine was undoubtedly equal to the best of the Médoc, though it has not always remained so. It is now considered, and rightly, that Mouton Rothschild, the head of the second growths class containing fifteen châteaux, is equal to any of the first, and certainly its price is as great or greater. Of the fifteen second growths, there are many names which are well known, the three famous Léoville wines, Léoville-Las-Cases, Léoville-Poyferré and Léoville-Barton; Lascombes now under American owner-ship and making excellent wine; the Pichons – Pichon-Longueville-Baron and Pichon-Longueville-Comtesse de Lalande; Cos d'Estournel of St Estèphe, a wine which is reputed to be scented with pines (but I must admit that my imagination has never taken me so far); Montrose of great and historic interest. There are fourteen third growths, eleven fourth growths and sixteen fifth growths, and it is among the fifth growths that one can expect to see some fairly rapid promotion when the long-talked-of reclassifica-tion comes into being.

It is now (1973), one hundred and eighteen years since

the great classification was made and there have been many changes. Most of the great estates have remained in good hands although there have been ups and downs. Haut-Brion had a long period of twenty-odd years of bad, or shall we say, unhappy management, but it is now back on the right road. Château Margaux had a bad patch from 1929 until 1947, but has recovered again. Other châteaux fell out of cultivation altogether, although I think most of them have been brought back now, but when a château goes out of cultivation, a good deal of the expertise and know-how goes out too and the vines have to be replanted, and time is not always on the side of the *vigneron* when he wants to resuscitate a good estate. On the other hand, there are some very notable improvements. We have already mentioned Mouton-Rothschild, but if we look at some of the fifth growths, we have names like Cantemerle which has been in the present family for ninety years, all good *vignerons*, and Pontet-Canet which, incidentally, is only across the path from Mouton-Rothschild; and Batailley; these wines will almost certainly be up-graded, perhaps even to second growth. Because of the improvements of this *Grands Crus* Classification, I am giving you below a list as it was formed in 1855; and afterwards, the most inspired guess so far (by Alex. Lichine) as to what will happen when the great reclassification comes about, if ever.

1855 Classification

Premiers Crus (1st)	*Commune*
Lafite	Pauillac
Latour	Pauillac
Margaux	Margaux
Haut-Brion	Pessac, Graves

Deuxièmes Crus (2nd)

Mouton-Rothschild	Pauillac
Rausan-Ségla	Margaux
Rauzan-Gassies	Margaux
Léoville-Las-Cases	Saint-Julien
Léoville-Poyferré	Saint-Julien
Léoville-Barton	Saint-Julien
Durfort-Vivens	Margaux
Lascombes	Margaux
Gruaud-Larose	Saint-Julien
Brane-Cantenac	Cantenac
Pichon-Longueville-Baron	Pauillac
Pichon-Longueville-Lalande	Pauillac
Ducru-Beaucaillou	Saint-Julien
Cos d'Estournel	Saint-Estèphe
Montrose	Saint-Estèphe

Troisièmes Crus (3rd)

Kirwan	Cantenac
d'Issan	Cantenac
Lagrange	Saint-Julien
Langoa	Saint-Julien
Giscours	Labarde
Malescot-Saint-Exupéry	Margaux
Cantenac-Brown	Cantenac
Palmer	Cantenac
La Lagune	Ludon
Desmirail	Margaux
Calon-Ségur	Saint-Estèphe
Ferrière	Margaux
d'Alesme-Becker	Margaux
Boyd-Cantenac	Cantenac

Quatrièmes Crus (4th)

Saint-Pierre-Sevaistre	Saint-Julien
Saint-Pierre-Bontemps	Saint-Julien
Branaire-Ducru	Saint-Julien
Talbot	Saint-Julien
Duhart-Milon	Pauillac
Pouget	Cantenac
La Tour-Carnet	Saint-Laurent
Rochet	Saint-Estèphe
Beychevelle	Saint-Julien
Le Prieuré-Lichine	Cantenac
Marquis-de-Terme	Margaux

Cinquièmes Crus (5th)

Pontet-Canet	Pauillac
Batailley	Pauillac
Haut-Batailley	Pauillac
Grand-Puy-Lacoste	Pauillac
Grand-Puy-Ducasse	Pauillac
Lynch-Bages	Pauillac
Dauzac	Labarde
Mouton-d'Armailhacq	Pauillac
Le Tertre	Arsac
Pedesclaux	Pauillac
Belgrave	Saint-Laurent
Camensac	Saint-Laurent
Cos-Labory	Saint-Estèphe
Clerc-Milon-Mondon	Pauillac
Croizet-Bages	Pauillac
Cantemerle	Macau

A Possible Reclassification of the Grands Crus Classés
You will see that the suggestion is to classify in five main

classes with a few, very few, given the greatest title of *hors classe*; above and beyond. The remainder will be increased in number – 69 against 60 – and will drop the numbered categories, substituting

Crus Hors Classe
Crus Exceptionnels
Grands Crus
Grands Supérieurs
Crus Supérieurs

Crus Hors Classe (Outstanding Growths)

	Commune
Château Lafite-Rothschild	Pauillac
Château Margaux	Margaux
Château Latour	Pauillac
Château Haut-Brion	Pessac, Graves
Château Mouton-Rothschild	Pauillac

Crus Exceptionnels (Exceptional Growths)

Château Beychevelle	Saint-Julien
Château Brane-Cantenac	Margaux
Château Calon-Ségur	Saint-Estèphe
Château Cantemerle	Macau
Château Cos d'Estournel	Saint-Estèphe
Château Ducru-Beaucaillou	Saint-Julien
Château Durfort-Vivens	Margaux
Château Gruaud-Larose	Saint-Julien
Château Lascombes	Margaux
Château Léoville-Barton	Saint-Julien
Château Léoville-Las-Cases	Saint-Julien
Château Léoville-Poyferré	Saint-Julien
Château Lynch-Bages	Pauillac
Château Montrose	Saint-Estèphe

Château Palmer	Margaux
Château Pichon-Longueville-Baron	Pauillac
Château Pichon-Longueville	
Comtesse de Lalande	Pauillac
Château Rausan-Ségla	Margaux

Grands Crus (Great Growths)

Château Branaire-Ducru	Saint-Julien
Château Chasse-Spleen	Moulis
Château Duhart-Milon	Pauillac
Château Giscours	Margaux
Château Grand La Lagune	Ludon
Château d'Issan	Margaux
Château Langoa-Barton	Saint-Julien
Château Malescot-Saint-Exupéry	Margaux
Château Mouton-Baron Philippe	Pauillac
Château Pontet-Canet	Pauillac
Château Prieuré-Lichine	Margaux
Château Rauzan-Gassies	Margaux
Château Talbot	Saint-Julien
Château La Tour-de-Mons	Soussans-Margaux

Grandes Superieurs (Grand Superior Growths)

Château Batailley	Pauillac
Château Cantenac-Brown	Margaux
Château Capbern	Saint-Estèphe
Château Ferrière	Margaux
Château Fourcas-Dupré	Listrac
Château Gloria	Saint-Julien
	Beychevelle
Château Grand-Puy-Ducasse	Pauillac

Château Grand-Puy-Lacoste	Pauillac
Château Kirwan	Margaux
Château Marquis-d'Alesme-Becker	Margaux
Château Marquis-de-Terme	Margaux
Château Poujeaux-Theil	Moulis

Crus Superieurs (Superior Growths)

Château Angludet	Margaux
Château Bel-Air-Marquis-d'Aligre	Soussans
Château Belgrave	Saint-Laurent
Château Boyd-Cantenac	Margaux
Château Clerc-Milon-Mondon	Pauillac
Château Cos-Labory	Saint-Estèphe
Château Croizet-Bages	Pauillac
Château Dutruch-Lambert	Moulis
Château Fourcas-Hostein	Listrac
Crus Gressier-Grand Poujeaux	Moulis
Château Haut-Bages-Libéral	Pauillac
Château Haut-Batailley	Pauillac
Château Lagrange	Saint-Julien
Château Lanessan	Cussac
Château Lynch-Moussas	Pauillac
Château Les Ormes-de-Pez	Saint-Estèphe
Château Paveil	Soussans
Château de Pez	Saint-Estèphe
Château Phélan-Ségur	Saint-Estèphe
Château La Tour-Carnet	Saint-Laurent

So much for the great wines, but what of the *crus exceptionels* (under the 1855 Classification), *crus bourgeois* and the little *crus artisans*? These are the wines that you will be drinking when you buy a simple bottle of Médoc, St Julien, St Estèphe and so on. They are all good wines, you will find,

if you buy them from a reputable wine merchant, clean, rich in colour and with all the character of a Bordeaux. They cost more, by and large, than other French beverage wines;, but they are worth it, always provided you have a good wine merchant. Just to give one last statistic, you must remember that the sixty great châteaux of the *grands crus* class only produce one-sixth of the total wine in the Médoc. It is in demand wherever good wine is drunk and there is never enough of it. You must expect to pay well for this wine, especially if it be château bottled.

The good years of the Médoc in the last sixty years (and I cannot think that you are likely to run across much older wine), are as follows: 1899 and 1900 were twin years of uniform excellence. Only two years ago five friends and I tried to decide which was best – we had three bottles of 1899 and three bottles of 1900 from the different *grands crus* châteaux. The result was still an undisputed tie, which was a great marvel. 1916 was a good year although rarely come across nowadays. All the 1916s I have ever tasted, including a Mouton drunk at the château, had one thing in common: a most marvellous bouquet, the most lovely nose I have experienced. 1917 was good, but is no longer with us, I fear; 1920 is now fading rapidly, but twenty years ago it was very good indeed; 1924 is going the same way, but in its day, was great; 1928 was one of those maddening years which has stayed dumb for a very long time, but it is now getting better and, in fact, is starting to develop amazingly after forty-four years, but I am afraid that most people have got tired of waiting and drank it too soon. 1929 has always been a great wine, but alas I fear that it is now beginning to fade and perhaps every other bottle shows definite signs of being over the hill. 1929 is however a very special year and many of the greatest experts including the late André Simon thought it was the best wine of the century. Of course, there is very little of it about now, but if you are lucky enough to find one, rest it carefully, decant it properly and you will know what it means to drink a great vintage. 1934, I think, comes under the heading of being perfect but uninspired; one cannot really fault it, but one cannot enthuse about it either. 1943 produced some excellent light wine which should be drunk if found; 1945 is being generally tipped off as likely to be the wine of the century and the yield was extremely small. The wine is big, strong and already with that lovely red-brick colour that comes with age to claret, but it is not ready to drink. I hope the pundits are right, because I have a fair amount of it waiting to become great, as I am sure one day it will. 1947 was an excellent wine in every way, and I don't believe it is going downhill, although it is unfashionable not to say so. In the last two or three years it has seemed to me that the Médoc wines are not keeping as well as the St Emilion wines in the year of grace 1947, and the Cheval Blanc of that year with Petrus a very close runner up if not a dead heat is one of the most magnificent clarets ever made, big, generous almost Burgundian but with that ineffable taste which is forever Bordeaux. 1948 appears to have been played down by the shippers because they had so much good wine from '45 and '47, and indeed at first it was a little dull, but it has developed wonderfully and it is now really very, very good indeed; 1949 is usually given full marks, but I am not sure that it will ever develop into a really great wine. 1952 is a good sound wine, but may develop into rather a hard one, which means it will keep for a long time and may improve, but may never become great. 1953 is a lovely wine in any context, soft, generous and good from the word go; this is the wine to buy and drink now if you can afford it; 1955 was also an excellent year, although perhaps better in St Emilion than in the Médoc. Among the other years you will find an occasional very good bottle from vintages of 1933, 1938, 1944 and 1957, but you will have to look for it. Of more recent years the '59 is excellent but unlikely to stay the course for ever. '61 is a glorious wine which will indeed last for many years and it is almost a crime to drink it now, although over ten years old, but if you do you will find it delicious, as is also the 1964 which should be drunk now because it is at its peak. 1969 was uneven and you will have to taste carefully before buying it in large quantities although it is very expensive because the yield was so small but the '70s appear to be doing very well indeed and, writing at the end of 1971, a very good opinion has been formed of their potential. What I would term the downright bad vintages, from which I simply don't believe there is any good wine, are 1910, '02, '03, '30, '31, '32, '39 and '41, and '51 should be if it were honestly made, but remember that the *vignerons* were allowed to *chaptalize* and consequently some of the wine is drinkable, but not really true Bordeaux. I personally think that they are right in doing this because if the wine is too sharp, it would be much better to add a little sugar and drink it in comfort.

The Wines of Graves

The district of Graves starts from Langon in the south and stretches for $12\frac{1}{2}$ miles along the west bank of the Garonne through Bordeaux itself, until it reaches the Blanquefort stream, where starts the Médoc. It is even more stony and gravelly (hence its name) than the Médoc and its production is much smaller. It produces some of the finest red wine in France, and some excellent but rarely great white wine, too. The odd thing is, of course, that the name *Vin de Graves* is synonymous with white wine wherever wine is drunk, yet most people would be surprised to hear that Graves produces nearly twice as much red wine of excellent quality as white wine of good and moderate quality. Take, for instance, the great first growth Château Haut-Brion, just outside Bordeaux, in the commune or parish of Pessac. Its wines have been famous for hundreds of years and it is mentioned in Pepys' Diary as Ho Bryen, and until it fell upon evil days (which in wine-making means that the owner knew better than the experts) thirty or forty years ago, it always made a fine wine of superb quality; a change of ownership put the matter right, but alas! a generation or more was lost. It is only recently that white wine has been made at Haut-Brion and in the opinion of many people, it is a pity, because the wine is no better than the best Graves white wine which is good and not great, and it would have been better perhaps to grow only the black grapes and concentrate on red wine entirely.

The principal characteristic of red Graves, and it is about red Graves that I sing, is what is called in wine jargon *finesse*. It is an extremely well-bred wine, slightly thin by comparison with the more full-blooded, dignified Médocs, but bright in colour, good to the palate, and with tremendous lasting properties.

I know something about Graves and its wines because I took one of the more famous of the red wine châteaux, Smith-Haut-Lafitte in Martillac, a few years back, for a month, and lived there with my family, and I saw a good deal of the country. Graves is just a little too arid and Château Smith-Haut-Lafitte is like many others. The prosperous châteaux are those being worked by proprietors who live on the premises, and in many cases work themselves. In nearby Château Bouscaut, where wines both red and white of the very first quality are made, the proprietor could be seen on his tractor, cultivating his vines, bare to the waist in the burning sun, while his family enjoy themselves at the seaside. I talked to him a good deal during my sojourn at Château Smith-Haut-Lafitte, and I got to know and like his wine, most of which goes to Belgium and Holland. His wine is classified as first growth and indeed it deserves to be, but as he says: 'One cannot let up in Graves; the production is too small and a bad year may spell near ruin. Nevertheless, the prices of wine have risen and a living is made.'

Among the great red wines, we have the great Haut-Brion itself at Pessac, and literally across the road, La Mission Haut-Brion, making a wine hardly less good, if at all; the Domaine de Chevalier, Château Pape Clément; La Tour Martillac – its 1955 is fragrantly superb – Lagarde, and many other famous châteaux all producing very worthy wines. The great years of the red wines of Graves are identical with Bordeaux, except that in 1923 they made some very great wine among which the Haut-Brion is still talked about with the '29s and other great years.

I find it much harder to write about the white wines of Graves than the red, but, of course, some very good white wines are made, although I have never tasted a great one. Apart from a few châteaux who make some good wine and sell it as château bottled, most of the *Vins de Graves* are sold to wine merchants in bulk and bottled by the shipper, and it should be noted that white Graves should never be highly priced unless it is a very special bottle, because the wine just isn't worth it and this, of course, lies at the root of the whole problem of Graves. The production is too small and the price is not enough. One might well say: 'What do not the *vignerons* grub up their white grape vines and plant red?', but it does not work out like that. Graves is traditionally noted for its white wines and won't give them up easily, but communications have grown better, and the years when the Bordeaux exporters were sending us their *Vins de Graves*, when the vines of Germany and even white Burgundies were hard to come by, have gone.

Of the principal white wine châteaux, apart from Bouscaut which I have just mentioned, Château Baret makes an excellent wine, Château Carbonnieux, Léognan an extremely good one, as is also the Domaine de Chevalier, and Château Olivier also has a well-deserved reputation in this country. Château La Tour Martillac et Kressmann make excellent wines, both red and white, and a little wine is also made at the very lovely Château de la Brède at La Brède, which is a perfect example of a small medieval castle still preserved as it was when the residence of Montesquieu, the philosopher. Graves in itself is not particularly beautiful, but La Brède is an exception and well worth a visit. According to André L. Simon, the optimum output of La Brède is something like sixty-four hogsheads, but I have never seen it on the market, still less tasted any, in this country.

To finish this section on Graves I give you the *Crus Classés* by the *Institut National des Appellations d'Origine* under Graves.

Red Wines

CADAUJAC:
 Château Bouscaut
LÉOGNAN:
 Ch. Haut-Bataille
 Ch. Carbonnieux
 Domaine de Chevalier
 Ch. Malartic-Lagravrière
 Ch. Olivier

White Wines

CADAUJAC:
 Château Bouscaut
LÉOGNAN:
 Ch. Carbonnieux
 Ch. Chevalier
 Ch. Olivier

PESSAC:

    Ch. Haut-Brion

    Ch. La Mission-Haut-Brion

    Ch. Pape Clément

    Ch. La Tour-Haut-Brion

MARTILLAC:

    Ch. Smith-Haut-Lafitte

    Ch. La Tour Martillac

PESSAC:

    Ch. Laville-Haut-Brion

VILLENAVE D'ORNON:

    Ch. Couhins

St Emilion and Pomerol

A few miles above Bordeaux and just past the Blanquefort River, which marks the beginning of the Médoc, the Dordogne and Garonne join, and from thence to the Bay of Biscay become the River Gironde. If we follow the Dordogne from its confluence with the Garonne towards the source, about twenty miles from Bordeaux almost due north, it flows through the prosperous town of Libourne which is the centre for St Emilion, Pomerol, Lalandé-de-Pomerol and Fronsac. The St Emilion district lies in the hills above Libourne and the Dordogne in broken, rolling country, its vine-clad hills spread here and there. Its centre is the ancient town of St Emilion itself with its winding streets, uphill and downhill, its monolithic cathedral with its spire built on top, its château and its monastery and, above all, its vines. Here on this rolling plateau is to be found a similar soil, although not quite so bleak, to that found in Graves and the Médoc and some of the greatest wines are made from grapes grown on the so-called *Graves de St Emilion* where again we have that fascinating difference from one vineyard to another which we have already seen in the Médoc.

Wines have been made in St Emilion for the last 2,000 years and the records here are more exact, for the Roman poet Ausonius in the fourth century AD lived at his villa on the hills overlooking the Dordogne. There he grew his vines and there he made his wines and sang their praises. On the site of his ancient villa stands the present Château Ausone and the present vines are the direct descendants of those of Ausonius or they would be, had it not been for the phylloxera which caused a hiatus of some years in the succession. Nevertheless, it may be stated as a fact that the vineyards round St Emilion and especially those, of course, of the Château Ausone, have been cultivated for 2,000 years and the sum of the knowledge of viticulture is to be found in the people who now own the vineyards, cultivate the vines and make the wines. At Château Ausone, for instance, the *régisseur* or manager who retired some years ago was in direct succession from the eighteenth century – that is to say, father and son had been *Maître de Chai* for over 200 years; this, in the cultivation of vines and the making of wines, means quite a lot.

St Emilion is a very much more picturesque wine country than the Médoc or Graves and is therefore understandably patronized by tourists. In St Emilion itself there are wonderful opportunities for cultural and gastronomic adventure, or shall we say, experiment, for there are many antiquities of note in a very picturesque town and everywhere one is invited to a *dégustation* of the local wines and the local cakes, rather like our macaroons.

The wines themselves have most of the virtues of Médoc and red Graves, but they are slightly more fruity; their colour is deeper, more purple; they are big, good hearty wines, and if they lack what we might call breeding, they certainly make it up in other directions; they have a kind of honest voluptuous beauty which mightily appeals to me. Taken collectively – that is to say, St Emilion and Pomerol, they are the nearest Bordeaux will ever get to Burgundy, and I suppose that is as far as one ever wants to go. They are ideal wines to drink with redder, richer meats and game.

The classifications of St Emilion which, in all, contains perhaps 200 estates or châteaux, are comparatively simple. They are two first great growths: the historic Château Ausone and Château Cheval Blanc; the first from the vineyards on the slopes and the second from the more gravelly vineyards on the plateau. There are ten other first growths: Château Beauséjour (proprietor Dufau), Château Beauséjour (proprietor Fagonet), Baleau, Figeac, La Gaffelière-Naudes, Magdelaine, Canon, Trottevieille, and my own favourites, Château Pavie and Clos Fourtet. All of these wines are uniformly excellent and if the prices are not so high as their opposite numbers in Médoc, this ought not to be counted against them, rather to the contrary. Châteaux Ausone and Cheval Blanc will cost you as much as first growth Médoc or Graves and indeed they have some right to do so.

The cellars of Château Ausone and Clos Fourtet are both, as are some of the others, cut into the living rock and it is an experience much to be recommended to travellers (who must go to the trouble of arranging an introduction with their wine merchant) to visit either or both of these cellars and there taste the wines of the two or three vintages preceding their visit. In Château Ausone will also be found the wines of Château Bel-Air, which is under the same excellent proprietorship and, contrary to general procedure, is racked and bottled in the same cellars as the Ausone but, of course, the cellars are vast and there is plenty of room for both. It goes without saying that considerable care is taken to see that the wine does not get mixed! There are many other good châteaux in St Emilion which are well known and the *Appellation Contrôlée* label, or better still, the *Mis en*

Bouteilles au Château, the certificate of château bottling, will prove a good reference for the wine inside the bottle.

Pomerol adjoins St Emilion to the north and runs down to the town of Libourne on the Dordogne, and if one had to make a distinction between the wines, one would say that they are, if anything, certainly more generous than St Emilion; again this splendid ruby colour and again the charming bouquet. The vineyards are contiguous to those of St Emilion and there is little difference between wines of St Emilion and Pomerol. Furthermore, these Pomerol châteaux were near enough to share, with a few others on the other side of the St Emilion border, the devastation caused by the great frost of early 1956. This catastrophe occurred after a warm February when the sap had started to rise in the vines; then came a cold snap of unprecedented hardness combined with snow, lasting for some weeks, which froze the rising sap in the vines and killed everything above the graft. I well remember visiting vineyards later in that year when I was living at Château Smith-Haut-Lafitte in Graves and being shown by the late Madame Loubat, then in her eighty-fifth year and for sixty years proprietress of Château Petrus, the tragedy of the vines shooting from below the graft – that is to say, on the American stocks so that the fruit which came from them eventually was the American hybrid and not the traditional French, and useless for making the fine wine of Pomerol. Up to that year, Château Petrus had retained a corner of the vineyard planted with the original pre-phylloxera vines which, for some reason or other, had not been wiped out during the phylloxera invasion. These have now gone, the last of the very, very few.

Madame Loubat was not to be depressed by this, 'Well,' she said, 'in my long life I have seen a few devastations and troubles; I saw oidium, mildew and phylloxera; we have come through them all. I don't doubt we shall come through this, but I doubt if I shall see it.' She was, of course, quite right in both respects, for the vineyards have been replanted and she, alas, is gone, but never let it be doubted that Château Petrus has retained its title of first great growth of Pomerol. Madame Loubat was an indomitable character and because her vineyard was small and the quality consistently superb, she would never sell her wine at any lower price than that of Mouton-Rothschild which is, I suppose, about the highest priced of the Médoc wines. Her view was that her wine was as good and the price should be the same, and while there may well be two opinions about this, certainly it was good enough for the shippers and merchants of Bordeaux to pay up and look big.

The tragedy of the great frosts of 1956 was that they wiped out most of the oldest vines and the making of fine or great wines depends to some extent on the use of grapes grown on the old vines. Generally speaking, a vine takes five years to come into fruit; from the fifth to the tenth year it yields well, and from the tenth year onwards yields well and produces the best fruit, but probably the best of all is produced on the vines fifteen to twenty-five years old, and in the making of fine wine, a proportion of grapes from the old vines is not only desirable but necessary. By now, that is in 1972, the damage has been made good and the young vines have come into full fruit and the wine is as good as ever except that which was made from the pre-phylloxera grapes at Petrus, and indeed Petrus is making some very splendid wines at this moment. Not all the vineyards were afflicted; many were sheltered, others escaped the full blast of the snow, and so on, but we shall be well advised to buy Pomerols and St Emilions of good parentage, either

63

before 1955 vintage or after the 1966 vintage, although some very good wines were produced here and there before 1966.

After Château Petrus, indisputably the leaders are other important châteaux like Vieux-Château-Certan, Château La Conseillante, Château Certan, Château-Petit-Village, Château l'Evangile, Château Moulinet, Château Plince, Château Le Gay, Château Beauregard, Clos L'Eglise, Château de Sales, Château de Bourgneuf, Château La Croix, the numerous châteaux bearing the name of Figeac, and many others. The neighbouring areas, Néac and Lalande-de-Pomerol also produce excellent wine of the same character, produced on a clayish soil, soft, fruity with an agreeable bouquet. Lalande-de-Pomerol, which is rather larger than Néac, produces a wine which may be compared with the first growths of Pomerol. The best of the Lalande-de-Pomerol wines is certainly Château de Bel-Air, a lasting wine, and there are also to be mentioned Château de la Commande Ruis, Château de Loge Couzelles, Château de Musset and the Clos des Nouaves, all good wines.

The vintage years are much the same as the Médoc, with the exception of 1921, which was a singularly parched year, and the hills of St Emilion and Pomerol were all the better for the altitude, and produced some excellent wine which the Médoc did not, in spite of its early promise. The Cheval Blanc of 1921 was particularly good, and although it is now finished, it has a remarkable reputation. Generally, it can be said that St Emilion produces very evenly with the Médoc, for the sun shines much the same everywhere in the Bordeaux area and great years are uniformly great and bad years uniformly bad, and once again I must refer to that extraordinarily excellent wine produced in the great St Emilion and Pomerol character in 1947, some of the best

claret ever made, while many of the Médocs including
some of the first growths were of good but not extraordinary
quality.

The Little Red Wines of Bordeaux:
Fronsac, Bourg and Blaye

After leaving Lalande-de-Pomerol and descending to
Libourne, face north from the eastern or right bank of the
Dordogne and you will be looking at the vineyards of Fronsac, and after them, through Bourg where the Garonne joins
the Dordogne to form the Gironde and so north through
Blaye. The country is beautiful with its rolling hills and
here are made most of the little red wines which you will
buy from your wine merchant as simple Bordeaux, if not
under the legitimate appellation of Fronsac, Bourgeais or
Blayais, as the case may be. These are all good sound wines
and there are many prosperous châteaux producing wines
under their own labels, although rarely château bottled.
You and I will do very well to buy these wines for our
ordinary consumption; they will cost very little compared
to the giants of the Médoc and they have the character of a
good Bordeaux; good rich colour with that infinitesimal
touch of sharpness to the palate which gives a kiss to a
claret. Having said that, it is a little difficult to know what
more may be said, because they are not great wines, nor
even very fine ones; they are just very good wines.

Fronsac, Bourg and Blaye play their part in the dispensa-
tion of good, sound Bordeaux wine. There are no good or
bad years for these wines as such, because blending is
carried on to a considerable degree – that is to say, the wines
of one year are mixed with another in order to produce a
first-class average bottle.

The Fine White Wines of Bordeaux: Sauternes, Barsac, Cérons, Sainte-Croix-du-Mont, Loupiac

Graves may be said to produce the driest white wine of Bordeaux, and the sweet wines ranging from what we should call the 'medium' up to the luscious sweetness of Château d'Yquem are grown on both banks of the Garonne, starting with Cérons in the north, passing through Barsac, through Sauternes with its four *communes* of Preignac, Bommes, Sauternes and Fargues, crossing the river above Langon to Sainte-Croix-du-Mont and turning left through Loupiac; all the vineyards in these districts, which are extensive, make good sweet wines of considerable reputation.

The principle of making sweet wine is first to use, of course, the right kind of grape and these are almost exclusively the *semillon* or *sauvignon*. The grapes are left on the vines until much later than in other districts, and under the action of the sun become wrinkled, even to outward appearance, rotten. Having been left to the last possible moment, and when the grapes are wrinkled and brown, they are attacked by a kind of mildew, *la pourriture noble*, or the noble rot. It is in fact a peculiar mould called the *botrytis cinerea*, a parasite, which pierces the skin of the ripe grapes, takes off some of the water, but leaves the sugar, which in turn becomes alcohol in fermentation, and because there is a greater concentration of grape sugar, the wines are extremely good and sweet.

Throughout the village of Sauternes, or rather the châteaux of Sauternes, this principle is developed in its viniculture, and according to the château and the price it receives for its wine, the grapes are, as it were, processed. For instance, the greatest of them all, the world-famous Château d'Yquem, which is the first great growth of Sauternes and the sweet wines throughout France, allows the grapes to ripen on the vine, and during the vintage, the pickers are sent through the vineyard day by day with sharp scissors, snipping out only the grapes which have become wrinkled and over-ripe during the previous day, from which it can be seen that the *pourriture noble* attacks while the grapes are still on the vine. These single grapes are then gathered and pressed and the daily pickings continue until nothing remains on the bunch, and the result is the wine of great character, tremendous and unique sweetness, and with very high alcoholic content, rising to 15° sometimes in the first year. It is necessarily expensive and only châteaux of the reputation of d'Yquem can afford to make wines exactly in this fashion, but notwithstanding, there are many fine châteaux in these districts making splendid wine by harvesting the grapes in bunches when they are over-ripe and at a lower cost. Among the fine wines in the *commune* of Sauternes are Château Guiraud, Château Filhot (a daughter château to d'Yquem), Château Lamothe-Bergey, and in nearby Bommes are Château La Tour Blanche, Château d'Arche Lafaurie, Clos Haut Peyragney, Château Rabaud and in Barsac, the famous Château Coutet, Château Climens, Château Myrat, Château Caillou, besides many others. In Preignac we have the Château de Suduiraut and in Fargues, Château Rieussec, both good wines.

The fashion, however, is tending away from the older sweet wines and it is interesting to see in the last two years that the great Château d'Yquem has found it necessary to make and bottle 'dry' Sauternes. Well, it isn't all that dry and it is certainly a fine wine. It is drier than that bottle we know as Château d'Yquem and it is much cheaper; let us see what happens to it. There is one thing to emphasize with these luscious sweet wines of Bordeaux: the best of them cannot be drunk with anything other than dessert, that is, not with any pleasure. I remember being given in New York rather a special meal by a kind host who wished, for some reason, to give me the best of everything, and he served Château d'Yquem right through the meal from the melon, through the fish, through the roast and the sweet. It was not a particularly pleasant experience. Some of the Barsacs, I suppose, can be served with fish, but by and large they are certainly dessert wines and should be kept as such.

The *commune* of Sainte-Croix-du-Mont which, incidentally, produces both red and white wines, is chiefly notable for the luscious white wine not unlike those of Barsac and Cérons. Sainte-Croix-du-Mont is reasonably proud of its wines and the district is *Appellation Contrôlée*, but it is a wine which is not imported into England to any great extent, except under a general appellation. There are a few very good châteaux such as Loubens, de Lamarque, Laurette, Domaine du Grand Peyrol and the Domaine de Morange. They are all fat, luscious wines and the local wine control stipulates a minimum 13° of alcohol, although this is often exceeded in a good year.

The next district downstream is Loupiac; it is on the right bank of the Garonne opposite Barsac. Again the wine is all fruity and luscious, that is about the same as Sainte-Croix-du-Mont, and the principal vineyards are Château de Ricaud, Château du Cros, Château Pontac.

Good years for white wines are not quite the same as for red wines, and in the case of these rich Sauternes and sweet wines it is true to say that they do not last nearly so long. I have myself drunk Château d'Yquem of as far back, on one occasion, as 1869, but it was no great experience and an 1898 was a definite loss. On the other hand, 1921, which was an exceptionally good year for white wines throughout France, is still excellent, although it is well past its peak. 1923 was a very good year, and '24 and '29 coincided with the clarets in that they were really good years, although not so good as 1921; '34 was a good year, and 1937 was a very great year for the white wine, far more so than for the red; 1943 was a good year, and 1945, like the Médoc, is likely to be a very great wine indeed, although in Barsac there was a severe spring frost and not much wine was made; '47 was a good year, and '48, '49 and '50 all splendid; 1952 produced very good wine indeed, although that great enemy to the *vigneron*, a late hailstorm, did enormous damage in Sauternes, Bommes and Preignac, and in that year, Château d'Yquem made but very little wine; '53 was a very good year and also '55, '59, '61, '64 and '70 are great vintages.

The Little White Wines of Bordeaux: Premières Côtes de Bordeaux, Entre Deux Mers, St Maccaire, St Foy Bordeaux and Graves de Vayres

All these wines are made in the comparatively rich ground between the Dordogne and the Garonne Rivers. The region is the largest of the Bordeaux vineyards and it is probably one of the most picturesque in the Gironde Department. It is rolling country, furrowed by green valleys and small streams into the Garonne or Dordogne, and the slopes of the hills as far as the eye can see are covered in well-cultivated vines. Here are most of the white and many of the red wines which go to make up the straight Bordeaux which is sold at a moderate price by reputable wine merchants and which is mixed with other finer wines and sold at a higher price and under an only partly true label by less scrupulous shippers. They account between them for something like 40 per cent of the whole of the output of Bordeaux wines, or in round figures, in an average year, about 81,000 tonneaus, each equal to 4 hogsheads of white wine, and 53,000 tonneaus of red wine. In character, the wine is soft and slightly sweet; it can be bought quite cheaply, and it is excellent in hot weather served very cold indeed.

There is no point in discussing vintage or châteaux for these wines, although both exist. In this market, the wine is made and marketed to be sold honestly for what it is and not for what it might have been had it been a mile or so to the north or south on a rather different soil. I strongly recommend these Bordeaux wines which are red or white, and I hope you will ask your reputable wine merchant to let you have some of them to try. They will not cost you much.

THE NOBLE WINES OF BURGUNDY

The greatest wines of Burgundy come from the vineyards of the department of the Côte d'Or, which lie terraced along the hills to the west of the road between the Côte Chalonnaise, through Beaune and Nuits St Georges up to Dijon. Below Chalon-sur-Saône are the less important wines of the Côte Chalonnaise, and lower still the much larger wine-growing areas of the Maconnais and the world famous and sometimes notorious Beaujolais. To the north-west of Dijon and in a little pocket by itself lies the region of Chablis where is made the wine of that name, which has its own special character, rather unlike any other.

Burgundy – that is to say, the true Burgundy – which is a wine made between the Côte Chalonnaise and Dijon, has all the natural characteristics of a great wine and is made from vines grown in small vineyards, strictly limited by the nature of the soil. There are many vineyards to the right of the main road (travelling towards Dijon), but to the left of it, they come down into the road itself. They grow on low-lying hills which are stony and gritty, not unlike the Médoc, perhaps not quite so poor, but here the comparison ends because there are two major factors in viniculture of Burgundy which do not obtain in Bordeaux.

Firstly is the factor of proprietorship; in most parts of France, vineyards tend to be large rather than small economic units, and this is particularly true of the great châteaux of Bordeaux. During and just after the French Revolution, the Burgundian vineyards were cut up into small plots and handed out to owner-occupiers, whereas the estates in Bordeaux and elsewhere more or less remained intact. As an example of this, let us take one of the first growth châteaux of the Médoc, Château Latour, which has an area of 40 hectares, or round about 100 acres. In Burgundy, the Clos de Vougeot, a name almost, if not quite, as famous for producing wine of the finest quality, has no fewer than forty-seven different proprietors in an area of 125 acres. It is inconceivable that all these *vignerons*, be they ever so expert, can make wine of equal quality, and if we agree that the soil is the same and the vines are cultivated with equal assiduity, we still have the human factor in the making of the wine itself. Consequently, while we know that a château-bottled Château Latour is consistent with every other bottle of the same vintage, we really do not know from whence our bottle of Clos de Vougeot comes unless, and this is comparatively rare, the name of the actual proprietor is printed on the label, for there is little domaine bottling.

The second important factor is that of *chaptalization* or the sugaring of wine. The Burgundian vineyards are much farther north than those of Bordeaux and tradition has been reinforced by authority in that sugar may legitimately be added to the wine in fermentation in order to bring it up to a reasonable minimum of alcohol. Most of the great wines of Burgundy are reputedly made without *chaptalization*, but a great deal of it goes on; much does art come to the aid of nature in the correction of her faults. Burgundy is the favourite wine of those lovers of good living, the Belgians, and if one drives through Burgundy at vintage time many cars with Belgian number plates may be seen drawn up outside the *pressoirs* and the *chais*. It is said that some Belgians will buy up the output of a single vineyard (we have seen that there are some very small holdings in Burgundy), and they like to keep an eye on the *chaptalization* department. This may or may not be true, but it could be.

These two factors, then, tend to make the appreciation of Burgundy a somewhat more complicated business than that of Bordeaux where in general, everything is, on the face of it, more straightforward. Of the superb quality of the great wines of Burgundy, both red and white, there can be no doubt whatsoever. Their chief characteristic is not so much heaviness as richness, and if they are less delicate than their equally famous brothers at Bordeaux they have their own strong personality, and it has indeed been well said that if Bordeaux, or rather Médoc, is the queen of wines, then Burgundy is the king. Consequently, if you ask a man whether he be a claret or a Burgundy man, do not be offended if he choose the opposite to your own preference, because in point of fact he will have had many glorious bottles of both. It is, however, with the white wines where Burgundy really scores over Bordeaux, for the great vintages of Meursault and Montrachet are incomparably better, fruitier, bigger, more fragrant and, at the same time, more delicate than anything produced in Bordeaux. Château d'Yquem is something of an exception and Burgundy has nothing to show like it, but then Château d'Yquem is a unique wine in any sense.

So let us start our tour of the Burgundian vineyards at

Chagny, travel up to Dijon, then go across to Chablis and down again to Chagny, from whence we can look at the Mâconnais and Beaujolais.

Côte d'Or

Chagny marks the southern end of the fabulous Côte d'Or which gets its name, some say, because of the gold derived from its fabulous vineyards which lie on the western slopes on long terraces, and others from the glory of the leaves as they turn gold in the vineyards in the autumn. Both explanations may be equally true.

The southern vineyards are a little to the west of Chagny at Santenay and mark the southernmost tip. Good red wine is made here from *pinot* grapes and there is one vineyard, La Gravières, of special note, but otherwise the wines are really first-class Burgundy. North of Fontenay are Puligny and Chassagne which includes probably the greatest of all French white wines, Montrachet. As in the case of Clos de Vougeot, Montrachet vineyards are very small (the famous Le Montrachet, although only 7 acres, is split between eleven *vignerons* according to André Simon). The whole vineyard cannot produce more than 50 casks of 100 gallons; it is indeed a very rare, much sought after wine. We have here a vineyard with the gallant name of Le Chevalier Montrachet and lower on the slopes of the hill, La Demoiselle Montrachet, and perhaps it is not surprising that what I think is the best wine of Montrachet, the Bâtard, comes in between the two. Among secondary growths in this district is Les Pucelles which is in itself a wine of tremendous character. But undoubtedly, the Montrachets rank as white wines with the greatest in the world and in saying this I mean no disrespect to the next *commune*, Meursault, a little town with a pleasant small hotel in which I have stayed, surrounded by its vineyards, in which about twice as much white wine as red is produced. Again the vineyards are chopped up and it is difficult to find any particular one of them to recommend, but since all are of the best, we are faced with no difficult problem. Personally, I am very fond of Les Genevrières, but this too is split up among a few *vignerons*. Another well-known vineyard is the Goutte d'Or.

Monthelie, near the western end of the Côte de Beaune, is a small village entirely given up to vine-growing, but it does not make very much, all red wine of various categories and all good. Yet nearer to Beaune, are Volnay and Pommard, both names to conjure with among Burgundies. They are all fine wines and mostly red, with Les Epenots and the Clos Blanc being best known of the Pommards, and Les Caillerets, Les Champans and Les Angles being the best known of the Volnays. The Santenots vineyards are partly in Volnay and partly in Meursault, but are generally associated with the former.

Beaune, the lovely walled city which is the centre of the Côte de Beaune vineyards, deserves a chapter to itself. It is a place of great historic and considerable architectural interest and obviously not without a certain amount of gastronomic interest, too. A good many wines are made in the immediate vicinity of Beaune. The Carmelite vineyard has a particular corner named La Vigne de L'Enfant Jésus and the wines have been sold under that name for the last 200 years or so, and very good they are. The principal vineyards of the Beaune appellation are Clos-de-la-Mousse, Clos-des-Mouches, Les Bressandes, Les Champimonts, Les Fèves, Les Grèves and Les Marconnets, nearly all red wine although some white is made at Clos-des-Mouches.

But the great interest in Beaune lies in its famous hospital and the wine auction which takes place on the third Sunday of November each year. The Hospice de Beaune was founded in 1443 by Nicolas Rolin and from time to time in the succeeding centuries, grateful patrons and patients have donated or left to the Hospice vineyards all over the Côte de Beaune. These vineyards are assiduously cultivated, and excellent wine made and sold every year at the auction. They are named after the donors of the vineyard; thus in Aloxe Corton there are vineyards named after Charlotte Dumay and Dr Peste; in Beaune itself, we have the original benefaction of Nicolas Rolin and Guigone de Salins and many others. Among the white wines the vineyards of Goureau and Jehan Humblot are situated in Meursault, and indeed many of the great wine-growing villages of Burgundy are represented. The auction takes place in the Hospice de Beaune by candle, that is to say, the candle is lit and a pin inserted part of the way down through the wick; while the candle is burning the bidding goes on and it is the last bidder before the flame gutters and goes out who obtains the wine. Prices are universally high, as they should be, for it is very charitable business and the wine is always excellent, and although it must be difficult in some cases for the wine merchants to get their money back they will certainly do themselves no harm by selling these excellent Burgundies.

After leaving Beaune, towards Nuits St Georges, we shall pass through Savigny les Beaune, which is the most westerly *commune* and which contains well-known and excellent vineyards like Les Marconnets, Les Vergelesses and Les Jarrons. The best wines are grown on the eastern slopes of the hills to the west of the road. After Savigny come the famous vineyards of Le Corton and Aloxe-Corton, among which are found some excellent wines, especially in Le Corton itself. I have extremely fond memories of a little bin of La Vigne au Sainte of the remarkable vintage of 1919; the last bottle was drunk a few years ago, and every bottle seemed better than the last. Les Perrières is also a very good wine, and the famous Charlemagne vineyard is well known and rather bigger than most. There are red and white Cortons, which mostly come from the Charlemagne vineyards.

Nuits St Georges is a tiny little town in the middle of the vineyards and most, if not all, of its occupants depend entirely upon the prosperity of the vines. There is a very good small hotel there, the 'Croix Blanche', and I have had very good gastronomic treatment at the hands of the chef. The wines are almost universally good and if some of them are not so great as the giants of Romanée I shall be well content if I never have anything less. Among the Nuits St Georges Burgundies I have one or two favourites, including especially Vaucrains, which is nearly as good as the best in Burgundy; it is a wine of great fragrance and it is full without being overbodied. Murgers is another good vineyard and Porrets another; probably Le Saint Georges is the best known and a very good one it is too.

As we travel towards Dijon, our steps have taken us through the temple of the great wines of Burgundy, and now as we enter Vosne-Romanée we are practically at the high altar. Here are the great and magical names of Romanée Conti, La Romanée, La Tache, Richebourg, the home of Les Varoilles, which is sold under the name of Richebourg; the whole of these five vineyards make about 79 casks in an average year and La Romanée only $5\frac{1}{2}$ casks. I suppose the best Burgundy I have ever drunk was a La Tache, again a tiny vineyard of only a few acres, but it was an odd year: 1933. These wines from Vosne-Romanée are necessarily expensive. They are all, I think, bottled at the domaine and most of them by Domaine de la Romanée Conti, who take great care and get great prices for their marvellous wines.

From Vosne-Romanée to Flagey and Echézeaux where the vineyards are not quite so famous, but make wonderful wine, especially the two Tête de Cuvée wines, Les Grandes Echézeaux and Les Echézeaux du Dessus.

Now we are about to enter the walls of the Clos de Vougeot itself, a famous vineyard of nearly fifty different plots within walls surrounding 125 acres. The historic Château of Vougeot dominates the vineyard from its north-western corner and it is all that remains of the Abbey of Vougeot, built in the thirteenth or fourteenth century; many are the stories that are told about it, and it is extremely interesting and very well worth a visit. It is now the head-quarters of the *Chevaliers du Tastevin*, a rather theatrical organization made up of *vignerons*, shippers and people interested in wine, and since the chief function of the Order is the *dégustations* of fine Burgundian wine and food, it certainly does a lot of good, to the Chevaliers, to its members and to the Château of Vougeot itself. The original wine presses, and enormous they are, still adorn the great *pressoir*.

In such a large vineyard, it is inevitable that there are different qualities (if we can call them that) of the soil, and in fact the wine used to be classified in three grades, but it is no longer. It is necessary, therefore, to know something of your shipper and in this you must trust your wine merchant, who will buy from those of the forty-odd proprietors who make the best wine. Drouhin Laroze, Rhom Dau, Drouhin, Morin and Grivot are names you can trust and there are many others, but with Clos Vougeot you must be careful; above all beware the 'stretched', faked wine labelled 'Clos de Vougeot' and sold in candle-lit Soho cellars and country pubs.

The next village is Chambolle-Musigny and here again

are some of the great wines with some very charming names: the Tête de Cuvée wines are Les Musigny, and a favourite of mine, Les Bonnes Mares, which always seems to be perfectly balanced, round and altogether delicious. Among others, the vineyard with the charming name of Les Amoureuses cannot help but be good and Charmes is in the same class. Part of the Bonnes Mares is in the next village of Morey St Denis, which does not make nearly so much wine as the Bonnes Mares vineyard in Chambolle-Musigny. The other Tête de Cuvée wines of Morey St Denis are Clos de Tart, owned by Monsieur Mommessin, who takes great trouble with his wine, Clos des Lambrays, Clos de la Roche and Clos St Denis, most of which are obtainable domaine bottled. There are some nineteen or twenty other vineyards making excellent wine, but not in the same quantity.

Gevrey-Chambertin contains, of course, the great vine-yard of Chambertin, reputedly Napoleon's favourite wine, although this is by no means proved. By all accounts, Napoleon was not a great gastronome and paid little atten-tion to what he ate and drank, but he certainly demanded the best and I suppose that Chambertin might well come under that heading. There are two vineyards entitled to be called Chambertin: Chambertin itself and Chambertin Clos de Bèze, which is a part of it. No others can be called Cham-bertin legally, but seven of the finest growths produced in Gevrey-Chambertin are allowed to suffix the name thus: Chapelle-Chambertin, Charmes-Chambertin, Griotte-Chambertin, Latricières-Chambertin, Mazys-Chambertin, Mazoyères-Chambertin, Ruchottes-Chambertin. There are five more first growths and many second and third growth wines and all, of course, are entitled to call themselves Gevrey-Chambertin, which is the name of the *commune*. Chambertin is too well known to need me to describe it here, but it should be remembered that the quantity made is very small indeed, although not so small as the Vosne-Romanée vineyards.

Next is the village of Fixin, and the great vineyards of the Côte d'Or come to an end in that place, for there are not nearly so many vineyards in Fixin producing wine of superlative quality: Clos de la Perrière is only 12 acres in extent, but the wine is much better than many of the more notable names in some of the preceding villages. There are two other good vineyards of repute, Clos de Chapitre and Les Hervelets; Clos de Chapitre I drank some five years ago when I had three or four bottles of the 1919 vintage, and excellent it was.

These great Burgundies which I have just described to you are comparable in every way with the great wines of Bordeaux, but greater care must be taken in their selection and purchase. Never was there a greater need for a reputable and inspired wine merchant than with Burgundy, and at the risk of becoming repetitious to the point of boredom, I must press the point.

The great years for Burgundy vary from Bordeaux quite a little: 1915 and 1919 were both remarkable – the latter wine is still excellent, if you can get it! 1923 was a fine year; 1928 and 1929 of course; 1933 was good and 1934 produced wine of style and there were some 1935's worth drinking, although Bordeaux produced nothing. 1945 is a great year, as are also 1947, 1949, 1952 and 1953; 1948 lagged a little behind Bordeaux, as did 1955, although both are good. 1957 produced some excellent Burgundies and 1959 also indeed some of the best. 1961/62 not quite so good; 1964/66 can be excellent and '69 bearable. 1970 wines also appear to be developing well.

Chablis

Chablis lies to the north-west of Dijon, about 134 kilometres, and comprises a little pocket of vines which gives its name to one of the cleanest, driest and most attractive of the French white wines. If it does not aspire to the fatness and arrogance of the great Montrachets or Meursaults, it is still an extremely fine one, dry and pleasant to drink with, in the higher grades, a good deal of character. Chablis comes from a comparatively small wine-growing area centred around the tiny little town of the same name and is in very considerable demand all over the world. It is, I suppose, a most perfect partner with fish of any kind and I personally often use it as straight *apéritif*. It is not the cheapest of wines, but it is by no means the most expensive and there are strict regulations under the *Appellation Contrôlée*, laying down the standards of the wine. These are the four classifications:

1. *Chablis Grand Cru* or *Grand Chablis*
2. *Chablis Premier Cru*
3. *Chablis*
4. *Petit Chablis*

It is unusual for these wines to be sold under this appellation in this country as nearly all Chablis is imported through wine merchants who bottle it either as straight Chablis or under their own label. There are a few vineyards of importance from which wine is sold under their own labels and these include Les Clos, Valmur, Grenouilles, Blanchots, Vaudésir, Preuses and, more familiarly, La Moutonne, which is the name of quite a small vineyard of about 3 acres and has become so well known because the quality is very good that Chablis Moutonne has come to indicate a different type of Chablis from the rest, which it is not. After a *procés* in the French courts, the name of La Moutonne may not be used for any other wine except that coming from the Moutonne vineyards.

Côte Chalonnaise, Maconnais and Beaujolais

South from Chagny is the country of the Côte Chalonnaise wines, centred round Chalon-sur-Saône. These wines are, not unnaturally, rather like the wines from Beaune, to the north, but lighter. In fact, since they are grown on the southern slopes of the Côte de Beaune, they are entitled under the *Appellation Contrôlée* Commission to be called 'Côte de Beaune Villages'. The wines are made both white and red, and of these the red seems to be rather better, although I remember that some years ago I used to buy an excellent little Chagny at quite a moderate price, which gave me great pleasure as a change from Chablis. The vineyards of Rully, Mercurey and Givry produce excellent wine of a moderate quality and fairly moderate in price, and Mercurey gives its name to the wines of two or three other *communes* in the same district. Montagny also produces quite a good wine, but none of these are in any way great and correspond roughly to the wines of Bourg and Blaye in Bordeaux in respect to Médoc, although the wines have more reputation and are less dry than the Bordeaux.

The Maconnais starts at Cluny in the west and Tournus on the River Saône in the east and it comprises a much larger area, the vine-clad hills stretch everywhere and a great quantity of excellent light wine is produced in the villages of Cluny, Lugny, Viré and Vinzelles, most of which is sold under the general label of Mâcon at very reasonable prices. There is some excellent white wine here, Pouilly-Fuissé, which can be extremely good and has lately come into favour. It compares more favourably with the best white Burgundies than the best Mâcon or Beaujolais can with the greater red Burgundies. There is a good deal of competition in this and the Pouilly has had the names of other villages tacked on to it, but Pouilly-Fuissé is now protected and is more and more being sold under its protected vineyard or estate. I have recently drunk some excellent domaine-bottled Pouilly-Fuissé from Le Clos at Pouilly and from the Château de Fuissé at Fuissé. It is interesting to see how this wine has been developed from one which was practically unknown to the general public in this country at least before the last war.

What shall one say of Le Beaujolais? It is so famous and the wine is so good. Its names are lovely: Fleurie, St Amour, Juliénas, Moulin-à-Vent, and who has not heard of Cloche-merle-in-the-Beaujolais? It is the wine of Paris, which city alone consumes twice its annual output! It is the wine of laughter and good living and if you can get honest Beau-jolais, it is all these things. It is never a great wine, but it is jolly good wine and it is sold at a reasonable price. Some of the wine, when it is bottled at a château, and there are one or two even in Beaujolais, can be remarkably good and I have now some magnums of 1947 Moulin-à-Vent, bottled at the Château of the Clos du Grand Carquelin by Monsieur Thorin, which are not so very far behind some of the great Burgundies. Nevertheless, Beaujolais should be drunk and enjoyed for what it is – the wine that can be made well, bottled early and drunk quickly. There is a lot of it made and there will be plenty more where it came from, and if it is sometimes mixed with other wines by a disreputable wine merchant, let us never deal with such and put our trust in those who will deal fairly. Dates on bottles of Beaujolais are more likely to be coincidental rather than accurate, but the years equate with Burgundy.

Of recent years it has become fashionable, for some reason

which I cannot tell, to drink some wine of Beaujolais in the year in which it is made. This wine is imported to arrive in December or even in November, is usually advertised with much réclame and people flock to buy it and pay over the odds for it. Let us not doubt that it is good Beaujolais, but on the other hand let us be equally certain that it wouldn't be any the worse off being kept for a year at least before being drunk.

CHAMPAGNE

It is fashionable in some circles to call Champagne over-rated, but nothing could be further from the truth. What I suppose people mean when they call Champagne over-rated is that they find it too expensive or that it doesn't agree with them, or that they consider it ostentatious, or something else, but over-rated, Champagne certainly is not. It is the prince of wines and fully worthy of our attention. It can mean also that they are talking about cheap Champagne which may well be over-rated, especially if it happens to be somebody or other's private *cuvée* at 25 per cent less than usual price, which may come from the Champagne district and which may even be made by *méthode champenoise*, from the second or third pressings of the grapes, but more likely is made by a shortened process and in glass tanks instead of bottles, which is not, of course, the *méthode champenoise*.

Champagne is made from grapes grown in the Champagne district along the valley of the Marne, around Epernay, which is its centre, and stretching round the *Montagne*, or Mountain, to Rheims. In England and elsewhere in Europe, only wine which is made in this district may be called Champagne, and a recent case in the English law courts decided this point against the Spanish wine firm who were selling Spanish sparkling wine as Spanish Champagne. It is now held that this is illegal, and while our writ does not run over the Atlantic it may be considered as settled law here. If we study the pleadings in this case, we shall get very near to the reason why Champagne is what it is and worthy of being singled out for special treatment. Counsel for the Champagne Association said the making of Champagne as such, although not in sparkling form, had gone on for more than 2,000 years. It was grown on special soil – that is to say, one only suitable for the making of this special wine – and with variation in climatic conditions, it also makes for special qualities and flavours. Nowhere else in the world could such wine be reproduced, hence the necessity to protect purchasers who may well be misled by a name on a label into believing that the wine in the bottle would be something like the real Champagne. This could not be. Many witnesses were called, among them wine-making experts, wine shippers, writers about wine, connoisseurs and so on, and in the end the learned judge decided once and for all that Champagne could only be made in Champagne.

Along the low rolling, lovely hills of the Valley of the Marne, the vineyards stretch like a great tapestry up and down the hills; the soil is thin and chalky and is poor enough in all conscience, as the Romans found when, obeying the edict of the Emperor Domitian in the first century, they grubbed up the vineyards to plant corn which in turn would provide the bread, if not the circuses, for Rome. In the event, the Romans got no bread and the Gauls no wine because the soil is too poor to produce corn in any worthwhile quantity at all, although it grows marvellous grapes.

For centuries, the wine of Champagne has been made and marketed. In the Middle Ages it was called Sillery, which is one of the principal vine-growing villages of Champagne.

Because the climate is variable and they are very much the most northern vineyards in France, the grapes will not always ripen fully and it is for this reason that not every year is a vintage year – usually only about one year in three. The Champagne you buy from your wine merchant under some famous label is never the wine of a single vineyard, although it may be the wine of a single vintage year. It is always a blend of the wine pressed from grapes of any one of a dozen villages, quite unlike Bordeaux and Burgundy where it is possible, and indeed usual, to buy great wines bottled at the vineyard, which might be as small as 3 or 4 acres, like La Tache in Vosne-Romanée.

The Champagne system is for the shippers to buy the grapes from the 11,000-odd smallholders of Champagne (according to André L. Simon, only twenty-three growers have more than 50 acres, while 4,300 have less than half an acre each); the grapes are taken to a central *pressoir*, which may or may not belong to the shipper, and are then pressed three times: the first pressing is obviously the best one and is called the *cuvée*; the second pressing can never make first-class wine and constitutes wine of that class – that is, second pressing wine; and the third, of course, is very poor stuff indeed and only used for the cheapest classes of wine which are sold at very low prices. What is left after all these pressings – that is, the husks and the stalks and the pips, and very dry they are – is distilled into the famous *marc de Champagne*, which at its best is really good and at its worst is reminiscent of liquid razor blades. To return to our first pressing of grapes: after the first fermentation which in the case of a strong wine may only take 24–36 hours, the wine is run off into casks and shipped off to the cellars of the shipper, who will eventually put the bubbles into it and make sparkling Champagne. The cask will lie about in the courtyard for a long time and still buzzes away in quite heavy secondary fermentation although really, I suppose, it is a continuation of the first rather than the second. Listening at the bung-hole you will hear a sound like a swarm of bees inside the barrel. The wine stays in its cask for perhaps a year until it is ready for bottling on its way to become sparkling wine known as Champagne; let us see how this came about.

Dom Pérignon, the famous monk of the Abbey of Haut-villiers, just outside Epernay, is generally credited as being the father of Champagne as we know it, but this is only partly true. Dom Pérignon was for forty-odd years the cellarer of the Abbey and became a very great expert on the local wine. He could judge it, he could make it well, and he did both, but he did not invent Champagne. There always have been sparkling wines, and the bubbles are only effervescence set up by escaping carbonic acid gas which in turn is part of the process known as fermentation. Any still wine incompletely fermented and put into bottles will sparkle, I mean produce bubbles, but there must be a certain amount of art in this, and what Dom Pérignon did was to perfect the system, or rather, he discovered through his knowledge of wine and wine-making that the wine of Champagne had very special qualities from which the sparkling wine could be made better than anywhere else. He could not have done this, however, had the cork as we know it not been developed at about this time, for unless the fermenting wine can be securely kept in its bottle, obviously the carbonic acid gas will escape and there will be no sparkle. Many were the casualties of these early days, and indeed for the first hundred years or so of Champagne making, due to the fermenting wine in the tightly corked bottles. Explosions would go on all the time and a heavy percentage of bottles would be lost. The Champagne bottle today is the strongest bottle made, with a special thickness of glass round the shoulders, and a Champagne bottle is never used twice, at least, not for Champagne, although most wine merchants use empty Champagne magnums for bottling their Burgundy.

After Dom Pérignon, the face of Champagne was changed, and this is roughly the method that Dom Pérignon perfected and which is still used today in the cellars of Epernay and Rheims. When the first fermentation has more or less died out in the cask, the wine from the different vineyards and pressings is very skilfully blended by the *Chef de Caves*, whose job it is, by tasting the different wines in the cask, to make the smooth blend with the special character for which his firm's name is probably world famous. He is, of course, the product of a lifetime of experience and knowledge of the different wines coming from different *pressoirs*, and from grapes coming from different vineyards. There is yet another subdivision, black and white grapes, for it is often held that the best Champagne is made with a proportion of black grapes, and, of course, most of it is. We have already seen in the making of other wine that white wine is made from black grapes by removing the husks before full fermentation sets in; it is the acid set up in fermentation which loosens the pigment of the skin of the black grapes and colours the wine, making it red. So your *Chef de Caves* must be a supreme judge of what grapes, in what proportions, and what wine made of what combinations of those grapes, and again the proportion thereof of the different vineyards, which you may agree is no mean accomplishment. The vineyards of Champagne are split up into three classes, *premier cru, deuxième cru* and *troisième cru*, each obtaining the price for their grapes laid down for the particular class. This is a further complication.

All this is done before the wine is bottled. At the time of

bottling, a small quantity of what is known as *liqueur de tirage* is added so that in fermentation, it will produce just about the right quantity of carbonic acid gas to sparkle the wine. This *liqueur de tirage* is simply pure sugar dissolved in the natural Champagne wine. The bottles are then corked and clamped down but, of course, not wired, and they start their long life in a horizontal position in the great cellars of Champagne, cut out of the solid chalk, extremely damp and chill. Later they are moved into special racks at a position of 45° with the neck down, and the *remuage* begins – that is to say, each day the bottle is given a short, sharp quarter turn in order to unsettle the sediment, which shakes to the end of the bottle nearest the cork. The bottles finish up at the end of this period of fermentation in vertical position with the cork downwards so that the whole of the sediment is gathered just above the cork.

At this stage, the Champagne is sparkling, clear and pretty well fit to drink, but if it is moved about very much, of course, the sediment which has collected in the neck of the bottle nearest the cork will make the wine muddy. So the last part of the process comes into operation, that of *dégorgement*, and this is the process of freezing the neck of the bottle in its vertical position, so that the sediment is merely a frozen lump, and taking out the temporary cork, at which point the wine inside forces out the frozen sediment. Then is added what is called the *dosage*, which is the right amount of liqueur called *liqueur de l'expédition* to give the wine just the degree of sweetness required for its market – that is perhaps only ½ or 1 per cent for the English market, because we like very dry Champagne, and 5–10 per cent or even more for those countries which like their Champagne very sweet. The *dosage* is put into the bottle, its permanent cork is forced in and it is wired up and ready for the cellars where it will stay until it is ordered, washed, labelled and packed for despatch to wine merchants, and so to you and to me.

From all this, it would seem that Champagne can never, never be cheap. Not only is there a scarcity of the best grapes to make Champagne, but the crop varies enormously, and because of Champagne's latitude the grapes do not always ripen well and often the crop is all too small. In 1970, however, the crop was so enormous that the shippers knew not where to turn, and I have been told that even two of the great water towers characteristic of France everywhere were filled with wine for storage purposes, and there were wine tankers at every siding full of the wine of Champagne. The vintage was quite good and this tremendous crop of 1970 will enhance both the quality and the quantity of the Champagne shippers for many years to come. As a postscript to this point, I would mention that when I was in Champagne in 1961, with André Simon, and he was writing his book on the *History of Champagne* (Ebury Press, 1962), the price of the grapes alone bought from the grower at the *pressoir* worked out at 8*s*. or 40*p per bottle* of wine made from them, and this is only for the raw material before pressing, before blending, before cellaring, before bottling or marketing, before overheads, profit, packing, shipping and so on. Of course, lower qualities are much cheaper and only in the very best Champagne will a very large percentage of first growth grapes be included, but it is bound to be expensive, like all first-class wine. Today there are about twenty or so first-rate wine shippers, and these include:

Ayala	Irroy
Bollinger	Krug
Chas. Heidsieck –	Lanson
Dry Monopole	Laurent Perrier

Mercier	Pommery & Greno
Moët & Chandon	Louis Roederer
Mumm	Ruinart
Perrier Jouet	Taittinger
Pol Roger	Veuve Cliquot – Ponsardin

Most reputable wine merchants, however, have their own private *cuvée* which most people know as party wine, but it is fair to say it is not always of the first quality, although probably excellent value for money.

The great vintage years for Champagne were: 1899, 1900, 1904, 1906, 1911, 1920, 1921, 1926, 1928, 1929, 1934, 1945, 1947, 1949, 1952, 1953, 1955, 1959, 1961, 1962, 1964 and 1966, and of these probably 1921 was the greatest. It should be remembered that Champagne is at its very best from seven to ten years old, and after that, except in very exceptional years like 1921 which stayed with us for twenty years, it won't stand up. The best wines are now 1964 and 1966, both of which are superb vintages. There are many old Champagnes, but they are mere curiosities rather than anything else. Pommery found in the cellars a few years ago an old bin of 1898 Champagne which had been overlooked and in fact had never been *dégorged*. This was *dégorged* and liqueured slightly and wired up in 1953 or '54, I think, and proved to be in excellent condition, if somewhat dark in colour, and without the edge to it which is the chief joy of Champagne, but delicious and still sparkling.

This is the best place to say something of Pink Champagne, and possibly pink and red sparkling wines in general. There is no reason why sparkling wine should not be pink or red; it merely means that black grape skins are left in the vat for 24 hours or so during the first fermentation until the pigment in the skins starts to dissolve and colours the grape juice which is being turned into wine. It used to be fashionable to serve pink Champagne to the ladies, and sometimes with dessert, but there is no great point in it; it cannot possibly be any better than the pale golden colour of straight Champagne. You pays your money and you takes your choice – if you like pretty colours you can have a pretty wine.

Red Sekt and red sparkling Burgundy are, of course, well known and much frowned upon in snobby circles; I don't happen to like them very much, but there is no earthly reason why you should not drink them if you want to. It only means that the sparkling wine is made from red instead of white wine. Whether or not the red wine will ever make a good sparkling wine is quite another matter.

ALSACE

The vines of Alsace grow on the eastern slopes of the Vosges mountains just west of the Rhine, and a very wonderful part of France this is: the fairy castles on the crags, the deep blue-green mistiness of the mountains from which may be seen the full sweep of the mighty Rhine. According to André L. Simon, there are 440 parishes in Alsace making wine and some 30,000 *vignerons* engaged in it, which surprises me considerably because there is comparatively little Alsace wine available in this country. Some two-thirds of it, said Monsieur Simon, is sold in Alsace itself, or about 10 million gallons, and the remainder is sold in Paris and for export. The wine itself is a heady wine of considerable character and not to be drunk lightly; it is by no means a little wine and has a good deal of the character of German wine in it, because, of course, they grow the same Riesling and Sylvaner and other grapes as they do in the German

vineyards along the Rhine a few miles after the Alsatian vineyards stop, and, in any case, Alsace was in German occupation from 1870 until 1918 (and again from 1940–4).

Vine-growing and wine-making is quite a considerable industry and it is best seen in wine towns such as Riquewihr, a small medieval walled town where the vines grow up and into the town itself and in which every single person is directly or indirectly engaged in wine-making and has been for many, many centuries. It remains unchanged and unfaked; there has been no restoration and it has merely been kept in good order while the *vignerons* have concentrated, year in, year out, on their beloved wine. It is the only town in this part of Alsace which escaped destruction at the end of the last world war. I recommend Riquewihr as being the best place to observe Alsatian wines made in both the ancient and the modern manner; if you poke round the back streets and the cobbled alleys during the *vendange*, you will see grapes brought in from the vineyards outside the walls being pressed in the medieval presses, some of them hundreds of years old, by small growers who make their own wine. On the other hand, if you get an introduction from your wine merchant (or indeed, even if you don't), you may go to the Château de Riquewihr, which is now owned by a famous wine-making firm, Dopff & Irion, and there you will see wine made by the most modern methods and will be allowed to taste the wine and enjoy it. You may have a simple meal in one of the two or three small restaurants, and if you are wise, you will take away one or two bottles of the wine as being the best kind of souvenir, and you will have had an altogether memorable experience.

Open the door of a famous *vigneron* in a courtyard just off the main street, and near his great wine press you will

find this inscription: *'Des voix mystérieuses soufflent à notre
vin en gestation des histoires vieilles et éternellement jeunes.'*
('To our wine as it comes to birth mysterious voices breathe
stories old and everlastingly young'.) This is the true spirit
of Riquewihr.

The vines themselves are grown on 7-ft poles, almost as
high as hops in England, and the wine is classified according
to the grapes from which it is made, *Sylvaner, muscat, pinot,
Riesling, traminer and gewurtztraminer*. Then, of course,
they make wines of different character according to the
grape. *Sylvaners*, for instance, make a light, fresh wine not
very suitable for keeping and with very little bouquet, but
it can be quite delicious and it is, as a rule, rather less
expensive. On the other hand, the *muscat* makes a heavy
wine, not altogether to our taste perhaps, and not so sweet
as you might expect from the name. By and large, Alsace
wines do not run to sweetness as some of the German or
Bordeaux wines, although there are some very splendid
examples in good years. The *pinot* grape, of which there are
two varieties, *pinot blanc* and *pinot gris*, makes wine more
in character with the white Burgundies and some of them
can be very good indeed, although I never heard of a *pinot
gris* being used for Burgundy. The *Riesling*, as in Germany,
produces perhaps the best wine, for it is a noble grape and
it is the *Riesling* which is largely grown in the district
round Riquewihr and Ribeauville. *Traminer* and the
gewurtztraminer, another name for the same grape, is a
smaller and rounder grape than the *Riesling* and makes the
finest wine; it ripens earlier than the others, and in a good
year, when allowed to stay on the vines, produces the only
really sweet wine from Alsace apart from the muscat. It is
in the smaller vineyards reserved by the larger *vignerons*
for the special grapes like Clos du Maquisard of Dopff &

Irion that the *traminer* and *gewurtztraminer* grapes will be found and made into the very best wine. Generally speaking, the best years for Alsatian wine are bound to be the same as for the Rhine and Moselle.

THE RHÔNE VALLEY

The vineyards of the Rhône Valley may be said to start just south of Vienne below the confluence of the Rhône and the River Saône; they start with the Côte Rôtie, through Condrieu, Château Grillet, to Hermitage on past Montelimar down to Avignon near by, where are the vineyards of Châteauneuf du Pape, and across the river to Tavel, famous for its rosé wines. All these wines have considerable character and are fairly high in alcohol, 13° or 14° is not unusual, and they have considerable staying power. They are, for the most part, grown on the west bank of the Rhône, but some of the best of them are grown on the stony, shaly slopes above Hermitage on the east bank. The wines of the Côte Rôtie, the northernmost vineyards, are of pleasant character, not too far removed from Beaujolais which is, of course, rather to the north, and the wine is nearly all red wine, made from the *Syrah*. Côte Rôtie is perhaps only two miles long, after which Condrieu and its adjoining *communes* make a good white, or rather golden, wine, some of it of very good quality but only in small quantities. The most famous of this wine is Château Grillet, a vineyard of rather less than $2\frac{1}{2}$ acres in extent, but it makes some of the best white wine of the very special dry quality much valued by some connoisseurs although not to everybody's taste. Also, it is very hard to come by – and expensive. Again, these white wines are heavy and heady, and with never less than 11° of alcohol.

Anybody who has travelled the famous *Route Bleu* to the south of France will have seen the Hermitage vineyards on the great bluffs overlooking the Rhône, and for a mile or two along the road. It is inconceivable that vines can be grown on such steep slopes, and when I first saw the *vendange* in this district I could hardly believe that men could hump the great tubs down the slopes to the waiting tumbrils and tractors ready to take the grapes for pressing. They seem to enjoy it, however, these great men that come charging down the hillside like mountain goats, and I am told they have developed tremendous leg muscles as a result of this, and it isn't difficult to believe. I would not like to get in their way when under full load.

Both white and black grapes are grown here, and if I prefer the red to the white, this is purely a personal preference. You will not escape the names of the *vignerons*, as they are painted all over the hillside and there are plenty of opportunities along the road for a *dégustation*, some of which I hope you will take, but remember that the wine is much stronger than it seems to taste, especially if you are thirsty. A visit to the cellars of one of the shippers, like Jaboulet Vercherre, will be well worth while. Vintage years do not matter much with this wine. It is sufficiently near the south to be reasonably hot nearly every year, and in any case the *vignerons* are extremely skilful in the art of making adjustments to nature. But it just isn't that sort of wine. It is a very, very good wine without pretensions, and while it can be bought under its years, and undoubtedly some are a little better than others, I don't think it matters very much. I doubt you will find the neck label of a bad year anyway.

Farther down the Rhône almost under the walls of lovely Avignon are the famous vineyards of Châteauneuf du Pape, once under the ownership of the Popes of Avignon during the time of the great schism in the fourteenth and fifteenth centuries. Here the wines are slightly lighter in colour, but no less strong, and undoubtedly the popularity of this delicious wine is due to its quality as much as to the romance of its name and age.

Across the river at Tavel probably the greatest rosé wines in the world are made. It is a comparatively small community growing red and white grapes of different breeds and sorts, and in the finest of Tavel wine no fewer than five different breeds of grape may be used; one I know about and saw being made (and, of course, tasted) was made from three black and two white grapes, to a formula which had been handed down to the *vigneron* by his father, and by his father's father. I do not suppose it matters very much if the formula is altered a little, but the resulting wine is certainly unique both in its onion skin colour and its distinctive dry flavour. A little to the north of Tavel and on the west bank are Roquemaure, Chusclan and Lirac. Wines from here must be sold as Côte de Rhône, and very good they are, but they cannot make the rosé wine of Tavel.

Almost all the wines of the Lower Rhône are best drunk cold.

PROVENCE

The *vignobles* of Provence lie between Draguignan in the north, Brignoles in the west and La Ciotat to St Tropez in the south, and from them come red, white and rosé wines, all rather heady, and nearly all best drunk in Provence, and why not? The best of them are put up in a very graceful waisted bottle, sometimes with enormous birth certificates tied to the necks. The red wine is one of the few which takes no harm from being chilled – this is a matter of taste – but the rosé and white must be very cold. Vintage years do not count for much from Provençal wines. Some of them may be found rather harsh to our tastes, but quite delicious – in Provence.

THE CHARMING WINES OF THE LOIRE

I suppose it could be claimed that the vineyards of the Loire constitute the loveliest vineyards in the world. From Vouvray to the sea, the great river flows steadily past low hills, magnificent scenery and great turreted châteaux. A great deal of wine is made along these hills, flaming in October in reds, yellows and browns, but, alas, no very great wine. The soil is perhaps a little too rich, and while the Loire, like everywhere else, produces its good and bad years, there is not all that difference between them, and the date on the bottle is not really important. The range and variety of wines are extraordinary, and while, of course, different districts tend to produce the same kind of wine they do vary very much indeed over the course of the river. Here follows a list of Loire wines, from St Nazaire at the mouth of the river through Nantes to Angers and going up the Sarthe a little and the Loir, back through Saumur, which is noted for its sparkling wine, to Chinon along the Vienne, then through Tours and Vouvray and along to Pouilly-sur-Loire and Sancerre, and across to Quincy on the Cher River.

The wine from Nantes is the Muscadet; between Nantes and Angers are grown the grapes from which the Anjou wine is made; from north of Angers near the confluence of the Sarthe and Loir Rivers comes the Coteaux de la Loire. On the lovely hills to the south of the Loire itself between Angers and Saumur are the Coteaux de Layon wines and, of course, all round Saumur you have first of all the Saumur wine and the Coteaux de Saumur. Between Saumur and Tours there are the Bourgueil and Chinon wines, on the hills a little to the north and south of Tours, the Coteaux de Touraine, but Vouvray is made near Vouvray and a little to the east, Montlouis. Then there is a very long gap, as the lovely Loire wanders through the country until we reach Sancerre on the west bank and Pouilly-sur-Loire on the east bank, both of which make the distinctive wines of this area, including the excellent Pouilly-Fumé. Farther to the east again on the Cher River tributary are made the wines of Reuilly and Quincy. Here we have something like sixteen wines all made along the River Loire and its tributaries, all having their particular character and all extremely drinkable. Almost everywhere, however, the wine must be drunk young – that is to say before its third or fourth year. This is not to say it won't keep, but it won't keep very well.

In Saumur and round it there is a very considerable sparkling wine industry, and sparkling Saumur is very well known in this country, some of it under the trade name of Golden Guinea. In some cases, that is the best of it, the wine is made by the *méthode champenoise* and is very good of its kind, but the climate is too gentle and the soil too rich to be really the same as Champagne, and it is not, any more than the best Anjou wine can be said really to compare with the châteaux of the Médoc. A good deal of sparkling wine, too, is made by the vat method, and this is sold quite cheaply – good sound wine and very well as a pleasant apéritif.

I am not going to try to describe all these wines to you because I shall run out of superlatives and you will, I hope, have noticed by now that I try to avoid what I call wine jargon. There are some words which come happily to the tongue and describe wine very well, pretension is one of them. Well, these little wines of the Loire (I don't think the

growers themselves would claim very much more than this) are all delicious in their way, and quite unpretentious, and the best advice I can give you is to lose no opportunity of trying them out. Drink them as beverage wines, white, red or some of the extremely good rosé made along the Loire, drink them for what they are; do not expect miracles, for you won't get any. Expect, however, some good wine, and among the very best, Pouilly-Fumé made at the upper end of the river, which is an extremely good wine, made from the *Sauvignon* grape and not to be confused with Pouilly-Fuissé of Burgundy, which is quite different. At the other end, near Nantes, the excellent, slightly sharpish, most refreshing white wine called Muscadet, a wine which I much enjoy on a hot summer morning as an apéritif. All white and rosé Anjou Loire wines should be drunk really ice-cold; keep them in the refrigerator as long as you like for use when desired.

Above all, give yourself the tremendous pleasure, if you can, of tasting these wines in their native haunts. There you will drink them at their very best and in marvellous surroundings. Don't trouble to bring any back with you because you may buy the best of it in those countries to which it is exported after having been carefully racked for travel. In recent years the *vignerons* of the Loire have taken tremendous trouble to improve their wines for the export market and some of them like that prepared by M. Vacheron patron of Sancerre for the International Wine Society are superb. I would also recommend you to try if you get the chance some wine of the Château de Panay at Saumur which is very special. But it is to be emphasized that these wines are produced essentially as fine wines for the export market and prepared for travel. The little local wines are different, and you may be disappointed if you bring some home to put in your cellar for a month or two; no wine of this class is ever quite the same drink outside its own manor.

THE LITTLE WINES OF FRANCE

Good wine is made all over France except in seven departments; consequently, there are hundreds, if not thousands, of wines which we have not touched upon in the preceding pages. Neither can we, because they are not of any great importance in relation to the great wines, and in the vast majority of cases they do not get beyond the confines of the nearest town and sometimes village, or even farmhouse.

Languedoc and Roussillon (The Midi)
There are vast quantities of wine made outside the districts we have already mentioned and the most prolific district is that of Languedoc and Roussillon (The Midi), which is a vast district stretching roughly from Carcassone to the Mediterranean, and wedged between the foothills of the Pyrénées and the Massif Central. Here is produced most of the good, dull wine, so useful for blending with even inferior wine from other parts of the world and which can be seen along the railways in tanker trains and bought as the *vin rouge ordinaire* throughout thousands and thousands of *alimentations* in France, at the lowest possible price. The soil is rich, the grapes are big and it makes a vast quantity of wine. It is dull, fruity and heady and in its natural state is not always rough. It is the true wine of the Midi and has sustained urban France for centuries. It is quite unremarkable but is not to be despised. So much for the wines of the Midi which are mostly produced in Languedoc and Roussillon.

But in this area there are a few pockets where very good wine of a different kind is made, especially sweeter wine, for the *muscat* grape is grown very successfully in the

Mediterranean areas, especially in the Côtes de Haut-Roussillon, near Banyuls and Perpignan, immediately north of the Spanish frontier, and many towns and villages here are making excellent, over-sweet, or shall we say, super-sweet wine from *muscat*, *grenache* and *malvoisie* grapes.

Jurançon

Not very far from Albi and about 35 miles from Toulouse is the town of Jurançon from whence the local wines have very strong historical associations, although you are unlikely to meet them in this country. I do not know whether you will like them in their own country – they tend to be over-sweet to our taste.

The Dordogne

Many good sound little wines are grown along the Dordogne; the most famous wine of the Dordogne Valley is made at Monbazillac, but it is a sweetish white wine from the *semillon* grape and not extraordinarily to the English taste. A good many dry and even elegant wines are made near Bergerac, the home of Cyrano of that ilk, but they don't travel and should be drunk *en route* or whenever you go to Lascaux or tour this delightful country. You will find vine-yards in vine-growing villages such as St Foy-des-Vignes and St Laurent-des-Vignes up and down the Dordogne and you will mostly buy only the local wine in the towns and villages.

The Jura

I am not at all sure it is fair to call the Jura a little wine of France; it is a very strong white wine, sharpish to our taste and altogether masculine in character. Warner Allen has devoted more than a chapter to this wine in his excellent book on white wines, but I doubt many of us can share his enthusiasm, although it is true that the famous Château Chalon is one of the classic and rarest wines in France. It is not made at a château, but in a number of small vineyards in the Jura and has an affinity with the finest of fine dry sherry. It can be kept for years and years and years; some people say it ought not to be opened until fifteen or twenty years have passed it by, but better still, thirty or forty. It is not a wine you will meet with in England; in fact, I could not tell you of one wine merchant, large or small, where it can be bought, but if you are travelling through France to Switzerland, stop at Dôme, the birthplace of Louis Pasteur, and there you will be able to buy a bottle of Château Chalon to take away.

ALGERIA

Algeria produces a really enormous amount of wine of good, indifferent and frankly bad quality, mostly used (fortunately) for home consumption. The good wine is sometimes very good and the name 'Algeria' on a label is not to be despised; you are far more likely to find it in bottles labelled 'Beaujolais' and have enjoyed it, too. But it requires more knowledge than I possess to enable you to tell the good from the bad *outside* the bottle and here your only guide must be that much-vaunted person, the reputable wine merchant who will not sell the indifferent or the bad. Always serve at room temperature for red, and cold for white; all red Algerian wines are big, full-bodied wines, and the white are dry.

So much for the wines of France. I cannot but help having omitted 2,000 names – famous, ordinary and perhaps, in a few cases, infamous – but we have not done with the wines of France because they are an essential ingredient of brandy.

The range of the wines of France is quite frankly enormous, and the only advice I can give is: when in France drink the local wine for the experience, buy yourself a bottle of excellent wine if you can afford it (and fine wines are dearer in France than they are in Britain and America), and enjoy them all. It may be that you will get a bad bottle (and there is one such name that I cannot quote here for risk of a libel action that is a household word in my family for all that is bad in wine); take it as you find it, and you will do very well.

BRANDY

Brandy is distilled from wine; that is to say, the grapes are pressed in the ordinary way, the wine is fermented and after the first fermentation it is stored in barrels and later distilled into brandy. *Eau de Vie* or *marc*, on the other hand, is certainly not brandy, for this is distilled from the husks and the pips and the stalks of the grapes when every single drop of juice has been pressed, not once or twice, but thrice. This has a place in the literature of wine and drinking, but not in the same breath as brandy.

The finest brandy is made in or near Cognac, east of La Rochelle, and at Armagnac, which is under the Pyrénées, to the south-east of Bordeaux. The finest Armagnac is generally considered to be very nearly as good as the best Cognac, and I will not argue the case here. I am myself extremely satisfied with a good Cognac and the best Armagnac.

The wine which is the basic ingredient of brandy is made around Cognac from the oddly enough named St Emilion grape, which is a white grape of no special character, except that it makes the wine from which may be distilled the most superb spirit. Cognac itself is a comparatively small area divided by controlled regulation into several classifications. The best brandy is considered to be made in the area round Cognac itself on the south bank of the Charente and is called the *Grand Champagne* because the chalky soil has an affinity with the chalky soil of Champagne. To the north of the Charente is an area which is known as the *Petite Champagne*, of which Jarnac is the centre, and there is also another area called the *Petite Champagne* south of the *Grand Champagne*. Immediately round the *Champagne* areas are the *fins bois* or those districts which grow fine grapes specially suited to Cognac, but perhaps not quite so good as the *Champagne* districts. Farther to the west along the coast between the mouth of the River Gironde and La Rochelle are the *bois ordinaires* where are grown good, but simply good, brandy-making grapes. The grapes are pressed, made into wine, and in the next spring after the vintage are distilled in the stills of some 3,000 or 4,000 distillers belonging mostly to the *vignerons* and scattered up and down the Charente country, of which Cognac is the centre.

The raw spirit when first distilled is, of course, not drinkable by ordinary standards, and farmers who grow the grapes, press them, make the wine and distil it, cannot afford to keep it, so they take it to Cognac and sell this excellent spirit to the big brandy shippers who have vast cellars and blending vats. The casks of new brandy are tasted, stored, and when the time comes blended with older brandies to make the best possible combination according to the market and the price. It is true to say that about 99 per cent of all brandies are blends of different years, and the ancient date that you will see on your brandy bottle, such as 1849, 1865, 1878, can well be, as somebody once said, possibly the telephone number of the shipper or some other numbers of a coincidental nature. It certainly does not refer to the age of the entire contents of the bottle, for what happens is this: the new brandy is fiery and rough, not at all palatable, whilst old brandy which has been matured in cask becomes smooth and gentle. Obviously, as the years go on, there is much less really old brandy left in cask so a certain amount of it is taken off for blending with new brandy and the cask is filled up, or refreshed as they say, with brandy not quite so old, well, let us say a few years younger, but not quite last year's. Now it is the supreme virtue of brandy that if you mix a good brandy with one not so good, or in its context much younger, the brandy not so good or younger will take on the character of the older and better brandy, so if we agree in charity that the cask of brandy was made from wine in 1878 (a very popular number to see on the neck lable of the brandy bottle) it has grown old and it has from time to time been tapped and refreshed. Possibly it is very good brandy but, of course, there is not very much of the original in it; somewhat paler in colour than the real 1878 would be, but a judicious admixture of a little caramel will put that right and the result is extremely smooth, palatable and altogether excellent, so let us not denigrate it.

Under the new laws which control the export of brandy from France it is no longer permissible to put a date on brandy unless it is authentically the brandy made of the wine of a given year, and so we may expect to see rather less of the fancy numbers on the bottles than there have been in the past. The myth of Napoleon brandy, and myth it is, can be easily explained. Brandy does not keep in bottles, only in cask; that is to say, it will not improve in bottle, but only in cask because of the special oak which is used for the brandy cask and the fact that it is slightly porous, and in the particular atmosphere of the Charente, waxes in flavour and in quality from year to year and wanes in strength, so that after fifty or sixty years in cask it is usually put into sealed earthenware jars rather like Roman amphorae, where it cannot get any weaker. I have been given brandy in Cognac of 1830 from a cask specially kept for tasting and demonstration, and it showed barely 25° as against 100° or more of proof spirit. Napoleon brandy, therefore, if such existed and was still in cask, would barely be strong enough to emerge from the bung-hole, and, indeed, its glory would have departed. If, on the other hand, it had been put in the bottle which you may have before you with its neck sealed with an 'N' and its cobwebby dusty sides, it would lose nearly everything and would perhaps be rather like . . . well, I don't know what it would be like. If you are lucky, what you may have in your wonderful bottle is a good blend of brandy, the original cask of which may or may not have been laid down in 1811, but the amount of the original brandy in your bottle would probably need a physicist to calculate. The finest brandies are not the oldest and they are called in the trade 'early landed brandies', but they are all but impossible to obtain outside the trade. If you should ever see, at your reputable wine merchants or in the cellar of a friend a bottle label something like this, 'HINES 1914, landed 1915, bottled 1942 or 1943' then that bottle, if it be a genuine label, will contain the truly great brandy. But you may well die without ever having this opportunity.

There are other brandies which are interesting, such as old brown brandy, which was very popular in the second half of the last century, and is a combination of good old brandy with, some say, molasses added. It lasts a great age and has been unpopular for many years now, but its colour has little to do with its age and if you are lucky enough to

come by a bottle, it is interesting to drink. The brandies that
you buy in the ordinary course of events from the great
brandy people like Martell, Hennessy, Hine, Rémy Martin,
Bisquit, Courvoisier and so on, are classified first of all by
the ordinary three star which usually indicates that the
brandy is at least seven years old, and then as follows:

VSO or *very superior old*, which are usually brandies of
from 12 to 17 years;

VSOP which is *very superior old pale*, for brandies from
18 to 25 years old, most of which are certainly not pale,
though they ought to be;

VVSOP *very, very superior old pale*, which brandies are
from 25 to 40 years old, but remember in all these cases
they are blends, and how much is 40 years old and how
much 25 years old is a matter for some conjecture.

Other House marks like Hennessy's XO, which is the
equivalent of VVSOP, and Martell's Cordon Bleu much the
same, are all very good indeed and you may rely on the
name of the great Brandy Houses to keep up their reputation
for quality. There is technically no such thing as liqueur
brandy, which is usually a name for an old dark-coloured
brandy and which may or may not be as good or better.

Brandy should ideally be drunk in small glasses which
can be held and warmed in the palm of the hand, preferably
with a cigar in the other. Remember always that a brandy
should be aromatic, and therefore the glass is better if
slightly warmer than room heat, but do not let the glass be
warmed over a flame, which is merely an affectation which
ruins the brandy. There is nothing except affectation against
using the enormous *ballon* glass – and, of course, the fact
that you will leave most of the brandy round the inside of
the glass.

ARMAGNAC

All the things that are true about Cognac are equally true about Armagnac except that the districts are different, and it is not classified quite so sharply with names like *Grand Champagne, fin bois* and so on. The wine is not made from St Emilion grapes, as is Cognac, but from two or three different, quite suitable grapes – that is, suitable for the soil on which they grow. It is again something of a village or farm industry in that the *vigneron* will distil his own brandy, but there are no Houses of the size of the vast Martell and Hennessy, or even the medium-size Cognac houses. It is therefore quite possible occasionally to come upon a very special bottle of Armagnac, although this must not be confused with some of the enormous Methuselahs of Armagnac (and indeed Cognac) brought out by restaurants in Soho mounted on gun carriages and other contraptions. Armagnac at its best is very good indeed.

I suppose there is more humbug over old brandy than almost any other class of wine. Suffice it to say that I once saw in a mirror in one of the greatest restaurants in London a waiter filling up the VSOP bottle from a three star, which I suppose was his own special form of blending. Taste is the only thing that can save you from fraud, other than dealing with only people of integrity, whether they be wine merchants or restaurants; I have never returned to the particular restaurant where this happened.

EAU DE VIE AND MARC

Around villages of France, especially in Burgundy and along the Rhône Valley, may be seen at the time of the *vendange* weird Heath Robinson arrangements with great coppers and a chimney stack on wheels rather like traction engines, usually standing in the market squares. To these contraptions will come the local *vigneron* after he has pressed his wine, with the husks, the pips and the stalks which have survived several heavy pressings. This residue, which has the consistency you might expect of stalks, pips and husks with no moisture, is brought in tumbrils or on tractors and a receipt is given for so many kilos by the man in charge of the contraption which is a portable still. The tumbril will unload in the middle of the square, the *vigneron* will depart with his receipt and will come back in a few days after the husks have been fermented and distilled, and collect the correct number of litres of the product of the distillation which is called *marc*. On to this heap will be tipped the contents of many other tumbrils like the first and gradually it gets larger while the distillers work away boiling it up. Dogs and goats seem to like the smell or the scent of the grape-skins; I have seen them walk all over it, munching a little here and there – dogs usually just sniff and cock a leg, and I am credibly informed that it adds considerably to the flavour. Gradually the heap goes down, and gradually the large demijohns of *marc* are handed out to their owners. I once asked the distiller whether I could taste the raw *marc* as it came from the retort and he smiled and poured a little into an old jam tin – one sip was enough, for to drink raw *marc* is like drinking broken glass. Such then is the nature of *marc* and it cannot, by its nature, be very much. It can be kept to a great age, and in the course of time it loses a great deal of its astringency and fire, and the best of it, which is sold in shops, *Marc de Champagne*, *Marc de Borgogne*, etc., while never *very* good, certainly smells nice and is usually made, I believe, from second pressings to make it drinkable. The growers themselves, of course, have a very special *marc*, but this is made from what is left after the first pressing which is naturally a different thing, or even perhaps in the case of a great château making a little *marc* for their own use and for special and favoured guests after a very light first pressing. Thus I was once given some *marc* at Château Mouton-Rothschild which is certainly not sold to the public and which is marvellous, and it had nothing in common with the *marc* one buys in shops.

4. THE WINES OF GERMANY

The wines made in Germany are grown from vines which are the most northerly in Europe and it is not every year that the grapes ripen sufficiently well to make really sweet wine. This has always been so and throughout 2,000 years of German viniculture there have been good years and bad years, although it has been possible to correct, in a slightly artificial manner, it is true, by using sugar to avoid disappointment in bad summers.

There are four wine-growing areas in Germany: the mighty Rhine itself and its smaller tributaries; the Moselle and its tributaries, the Saar and Ruwer; Steinwein comes from Würzburg or the region of Würzburg in Franconia; and Baden and Württemburg where a large amount of red wine, not of the first quality, is made. The classic wines all come from the low hills through which the Rhine flows and the steeper hills along the Moselle. Touristically, there could be no better trip than to drive from, say, Saarburg or Trier in the upper Moselle, along the lovely winding hills with the vineyards falling straight into the river as far as Enkirch, and crossing the hills to Lorch on the Rhine and driving down through Bingen, and Mainz to Worms or even farther south. The scenery is delightful, the romantic castles of the Rhine nearly always in view, the people are friendly and the wine, which is in plentiful supply, delicious, and, indeed, cheap.

In discussing German wine, however, it is necessary to know something of the extraordinary refinement to which the German *vigneron* has brought his art and to understand something also of the odd polysyllabic words appearing on the labels of the bottles. They are worth learning, and, of course, they are most important in so far as they refer to the contents of the bottle. German wines can be literally the most expensive in the world, that is to say, *some* German wine; I myself saw (but did not buy) in a Frankfurt restaurant wine list a Schloss Johannisburger Trocken-beerenauslese 1937 at no less than DM.200, or £25, per bottle. Obviously there are not many wines in this class, and in order to find out how this may come about, we must learn something of the German wine nomenclature.

The ordinary wine of the country – that is, the wine of any village or farmyard – can be called in the first place by

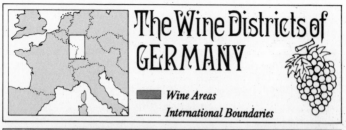

The Wine Districts of
GERMANY

Wine Areas

.... International Boundaries

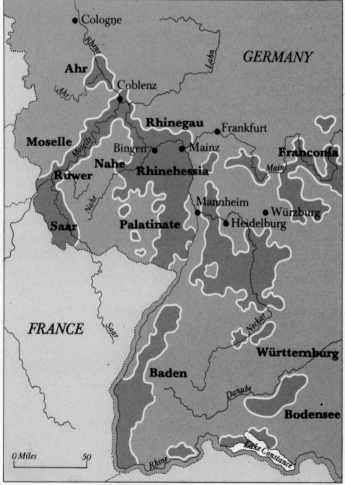

● Cologne

Rhine

Lahn

GERMANY

Ahr

Ahr

Coblenz

Rhinegau

Frankfurt ●

Moselle

Moselle

Bingen ●

Mainz ●

Nahe

Rhinehessia

Franconia

Main

Ruwer

Nahe

Mannheim

● Würzburg

Saar

Palatinate

● Heidelburg

FRANCE

Saar

Neckar

Württemburg

Baden

Danube

Bodensee

0 Miles   50

Rhine

Lake Constance

the name of the village. Let us take one of the best of the Moselle wines: Bernkastel. The common wine of this area will be called Bernkasteler, then if it is from a particular vineyard like the famous Doktor vineyard it will be called Bernkasteller Doktor, so the second name is the name of the vineyard. It is usual to follow this with the date, which might be 1960er.

So much for the ordinary and excellent wines. Then we start into some rather special classes, perhaps where the grapes have been carefully picked out or selected as fully ripe with no mildewed bunches, thus ensuring a very clear, sweet wine, and this wine (which may not, by law, be sweetened) is called *Auslese* or 'selected'. Another special class is the wine made from late gathered rather than over-ripe grapes, and is called *spätlese*, which is even better still, and both these may be called *fein* or *feinste*, indicating yet a special quality of *auslese* or *spätlese*. Above this, there are *goldbeerenauslese*, made from over-ripe individual grapes cut from the bunch in their perfection, until we finally get to the great *trockenbeerenauslese*, which is made only in the hottest years from very, very over-ripe grapes, picked singly, and upon which the *pourriture noble* has already formed. Some growers are said to take only the juice pressed out of the rotten grapes by the weight of the equally rotten grapes above; at least this would explain the price of the wine. The words 'Cabinet Wine' mean that it is a bottle from the grower's special reserve or 'cabinet'; or *Fuder No. 61* (or some other number) which means that it came from a very special barrel or *fuder*. The only other thing you need to understand is the description on the label as to whether the wine is *natur* or *naturrein*, a description laid down by law for wine which is pure, unblended and unsugared. There are other words like *wachstum* or *ohnesnaem original abfelung*, which means that it is bottled at the place of origin, *weingut* which really means that it comes from the person named on the label, but does not necessarily mean that it is bottled at that place and it may indeed be English bottled, and none the worse for that. In later years, the wines of Germany have tended to be drunk younger and younger and this is largely due to new technical processes employed in filtering, racking and timing to expedite the slow natural process. Some people, including the greatest experts, think that great wines cannot properly be made this way, and I think it improbable that the greatest wines are, but it is certainly true that the vast majority of German wine is made in hygienically impeccable press-houses and fermenting vats by most modern processes. The wine is absolutely delicious, and provided you do not run the risk of keeping it over the years (there would appear to be little point in this), I think the wine can only be helped by modern aids in its making. Since it is now fashionable for German wines to be drunk in the year after, and certainly within three years of making, we have nothing much to worry about.

The general procedure in Germany is for the grower to make his own wine and the standard barrel in which the wine is contained is called the *fuder* on the Moselle and some parts of the Palatinate, which corresponds roughly to our tun and contains 960 litres. On the Rhine, the barrel is called a *stück*, and contains 1,200 litres. The *fuders* or *stücken* of wine are then laid by in a cellar and auctions take place throughout the wine-growing districts during the winter months. The wine is bought and sold largely through brokers, by the great wine shipping firms in Bernkastel, Mainz, Worms, Bingen and in various other larger wine villages in the middle of the vineyards. Sometimes a *fuder* of specially good wine is kept by the grower for a year or two and sold at a much higher price, but most of it is disposed of in the normal way of trade and is bottled, labelled and shipped mostly, of course, in Germany, but a great amount to this country to famous Rhine names like Deinhard, Hallgarten, Langenbach and Loeb, who are the principal shippers today. Some of the wine is bottled on the estate or domaine and this is always carefully labelled with the half-dozen or so other involved jaw-cracking German names which we have previously discussed.

German wine starts life as the palest of pale gold, an infinitely lovely shade of primrose, and as it gets older it gets darker, and on the last occasion I had the privilege of drinking a 1921 Trockenbeerenauslese it had become as dark as Olorosa sherry, and the edge had gone off its sweetness, but it was still very good.

Rhine wines are always called Hock and this is derived from Hochheim, which is roughly in between Mainz and Wiesbaden, and contains fine vineyards. In the early years of Queen Victoria very little Rhenish wine was sent to England, but with the advent of the Prince Consort a few *stücken* were shipped, and became very popular. Queen Victoria, who had decided preferences in most things, thought that the best of it came from Hochheim, and as is usual when the Crown expresses its opinion this wine became tremendously popular, and, of course, Hochheim could not produce enough of it, so it gradually gave its name to the wine generally along that part of the Rhine, which is called Rheingau and which does in fact, produce the greatest of all the Hocks.

Now, the German wine regulations which, if anything, are stricter than the French, would not allow any wine other than that from Hochheim to be labelled under that name. So we have the Rhine wines, and those of its tributary the Nahe, known as Hock, and the wine of the Moselle and its tributaries, the Ruwer and the Saar and the Sauer, which are called Moselles, and if you want to get a reputation for knowing the difference between them, remember that the Rhine wines, or Hocks, are always sold in brown bottles and Moselles are always sold in green bottles: so to make an impression, just observe the colour of the bottle from which the wine is being served. In point of fact, there is quite a difference between the two wines, which, with a little cultivation, you will soon become proficient in noticing. The Moselle wines are just a little more light and charming, or as the Germans say, *spritlig*, which means sprightly, but which does not mean sparkling – it means the wine is lively. The great German Hocks have a certain dignity; they are serious wines and the little Moselles chuck them neatly under the chin and run away laughing.

There are more than thirty different types of grape used throughout the German vineyards according to the type of wine and the district. Probably the *Sylvaner* is the most planted vine, but it is the famous white *Riesling* grape which makes the great Hocks and Moselles. This vine produces small, tight bunches of golden grapes, and rivals even the mighty *Pinot blanc* of Champagne and Burgundy for its wine-making properties. The *Traminer, Rulaender Elbing,* and *muscatel* grapes are also widely grown and used, and there is a great deal of experimental and development work going on with cross-breeds of vine, some of which have had considerable success, like the *Mueller-Thurgau* which is a cross between the *Riesling* and the *Sylvaner*.

The first of the great German Rhine wine districts is the Rheingau – that is to say, vineyards on the east bank of the Rhine between Lorch and Mainz. There are, of course, one

121

or two small vineyards or wine towns on the west bank, but the main towns and vineyards are on the east, and here we have the classic Schloss Johannisberg, which is still in the Metternich family and has been for nearly 200 years, and what may be even a greater one, Schloss Vollrads. Both of these famous vineyards make and bottle their own wine, Schloss Johannisberg under Prince Metternich and Vollrads under Prince Henry of Prussia. There are a few others doing the same thing, but generally the wine is made and sold by the smaller growers in autumn or by private bargain.

The Rheingau really starts with St Goarshausen, comes down to Kaub, which is somewhat inland, then to Lorch which marks the beginning of the great vineyards, Assmannshausen, Rudesheim, which has developed into something like a Rhine wine resort – Brighton on the Rhine. Good hotels are found in Rudesheim, and indeed all along the Rhine, and it has become something of a holiday centre where there is always plenty to see with the great life of the Rhine, its steamers, its enormous barges, its pleasure-boats plying busily up and down, the vineyards and the forests at the back of the hills to visit, and, above all, there is the famous Throsselgasse or the Street of the Thrushes, a comparatively short and narrow street lined on both sides with enormous German wine cellars with wonderful bands and where singing and dancing go on all the time, while pretty *fraus* rush backwards and forwards with the wine. There is a good deal of competition between wine *kellers* and a good deal of competition between the Germans who drink the wine. As one bottle is disposed of and another brought, the empty is stood in the middle of the table, and towards morning when the night is far spent there is very little of the table left showing in some cases. Yes, the

Throsselgasse is quite an experience and I recommend it to you. After Rudesheim, Geisenheim and Winkel, Mittelheim, Oestrich, Hattenheim and Erbach, while just over the hills from the Rhine are Hallgarten, Keidrich, Martinstal and Rhauenthal. These are all famous names and each of them has many equally famous vineyards of which you may learn quite easily from longer books than this. But from this district come some of the greatest wines in Germany and, of their kind, the greatest in the world.

Along the Rhine between Bingen and Worms are the original vineyards of the Rhinehesse in a great horseshoe made by the Rhine and the Nahe. Worms is the centre of the Rheinhesse, which contains many famous names which you may have pondered over on the complicated labels, such as:

Bodenheim	Deinheim	Bickelheim
Wachenheim	Wintersblum	Ockenheim
Nierstein	Alsheim	Urleschaum
Oppenheim		

and many other smaller villages.

Many famous wine houses have their headquarters in the lovely city of Worms near where, it will be remembered, the Rhine maidens still guard the Nibelungen treasure which was thrown into the river off Worms. Worms is inseparable from Liebfraumilch about which so many stories are told, but the true story of Liebfraumilch is not unlike that of Hock, only very much older. Just as Hock derives from the town of Hochheim, so the Liebfraumilch derives from the Church of Our Lady in Worms which, in the Middle Ages, was a monastery and contained, as monasteries usually do, monks, who were also extremely good makers of wine, rather like Dom Pérignon at Hautvilliers. The monks cultivated their vines which did, and in fact still do, grow right up to the walls of the church itself, and such was their industry and expertise that over the years the wine made by the monks became famous throughout the length and breadth of the land, and, of course, it was called *Liebfraumilch*, which simply means the milk of the Church of Our Lady and does not mean, in this context, sweet mother's milk or anything so silly. Like Hock, soon there was not nearly enough wine from the vineyards of Our Lady's church to supply the demand and, consequently, the local growers and exporters soon matched the wine, or tried to, with wine of a similar standard and dubbed it all Liebfraumilch, and so it still goes everywhere to the uttermost ends of the earth as being a popular and rather sweet wine of moderate price and a wine which can be drunk with most things. Now the true Liebfraumilch can still be made and still be bought, but does not call itself Liebfraumilch; it is called Liebfrauen*stift*, which means the Church Piece, or the church plot, and there the original vineyards are still cultivated with extreme care by the three people who own them, one of whom is Langenbach. The wine made from the grapes grown on the Liebfrauenstift is extremely rare and hard to come by – there is very little of it – it is supremely delicate and charming, so delicate indeed that I do not think it should be drunk with food at all, but purely on its own merit by people who love fine wine, with nothing more than a dry biscuit. All this, however, does nothing to denigrate the great name of Liebfraumilch which has its place on the dinner tables of the world and in the hands of your reputable wine merchant, it will give you nothing but pleasure in the right place.

The third great wine district of the Rhine proper is the Palatinate or the Rheinpfalz. This is south of Worms and the low-lying hills to the west, and contains famous names like Dürkheid, Niederkirchen, Diedesheim, Königsbach, Deidesfeld, Edenkoben and so on. The Palatinate has been developed for wine growing since Roman times and particularly under the electoral princes of the Palatinate during the hey-day of the Holy Roman Empire, and indeed it went too far and wine growing had to be stopped, or rather, further extensions of the vineyards had to be stopped because of over-production and the consequent lowering of quality. Actually, the Palatinate still produces a greater quantity of wine than any of the Rhine vineyards or wine-growing provinces; the climate is milder than in the more northern areas and the soil rather better and, considered as a whole, produces good clean wines of general average quality, which should be reasonable in price although, of course, one will always find the exception of a remarkable *stück* from one of the great vineyards.

THE MOSELLE, SAAR AND RUWER VALLEYS

Where the Luxemburg vineyards leave off, the German vineyards begin, starting at Wasserbillig, going on through Treves or Trier, through such famous names as Piesport to Bernkastel, and finishing as far as viticulture is concerned, somewhere near Enkirch, but with a good many vineyards in between there and the confluence with the Rhine at Koblenz. The particular characteristics of these Moselles were commented on with considerable approval by that wine-loving Roman, Ausonius (of Château Ausone in St Emilion) who lived in the Roman town of Trier for some years and who not only drank and enjoyed the wine but wrote poetry about it too; no very difficult thing, I hasten to add. I personally find it extremely difficult to make heavy weather in terms of being able to distinguish a wine of one village from another; in fact, I cannot. If they are well made, they are delicious and they usually are well made. Some are better than others, and some are considerably more expensive. You cannot expect, and of course this is true of many other wines besides Moselle, to buy the finest wines cheaply, but you can, with Moselle, buy an extraordinarily good wine at a reasonable price. If you pay too little, you may find them sharpish; you can buy your Moselle from modest prices to whatever you like, for there are many giants.

Probably the most famous vineyard along the Moselle is the Doktor vineyard at Bernkastel, quite a large vineyard divided between three growers and like most Moselle vineyards, on very, very steep, shaley, gritty slopes, which makes things difficult for the gatherers at the time of the vintage. The grapes are gathered with great care, and, when the weather permits great vintages are made and I would not like to know how many times one hears the joke over a bottle of Bernkastel Doktor from one's host that, 'My doctor lives in Bernkastel'. It is probably quite true, too. The Doktor vineyard is named after its original proprietor, Dr Thanisch who, by supreme cultivation and application brought it to its well-deserved fame. From Bernkastel, it is not very far to Wehlen renowned for its famous Sonnenuhr vineyard where some of the finest wines of Moselle are made, and on the other, or Rhine side of the town to Zeltingen, Piesport, Trabach and Traben, through the most glorious scenery, with an occasional castle, and always the Moselle winding round and round through the steep vineyards. Here you may, in one of the many small riverside restaurants, which are not pretentious or expensive, have a delicious light lunch of trout caught that morning in the Moselle and washed down by the *ordinaire* of the district. which is more likely to be *extraordinaire* under these conditions.

OTHER GERMAN WINES

The wines of the Middle Rhine are made north of the Rheingau above Koblenz and west of the Ahr, slightly to the west of the same district. They are generally good, clean, ordinary wines which are better than they used to be. The wines of Baden and Württemburg are made between Apventol down past Freiburg nearly to the Swiss frontier, and here are grown most of the German red wines which are also not particularly remarkable but seem quite good, especially if drunk where they are made. A good deal of local red wine is made round Lake Constance.

The only other considerable wine district in Germany is the white Franconia wine area, popularly known as Stein-wein. It is made rather to the east of the Rhine in Main valley, the district round Würzburg due east of Mainz and on the River Main. 'Steinwein in Bocksbeutel' is very well known in most parts of the world; the bocksbeutel is a squat flagon which has always been the vessel for the wines of Franconia, and the wine itself is extremely strong, very good, but sometimes a little sharpish. I cannot go as far as the late Morton Shand who says in *A Book of Wine*:

> *There is a sort of family resemblance between all German wines which may be called, for lack of a better phrase, a sort of vernal floweriness. This characteristic steinwein possesses in a greater degree than any of its fellows. It has a bland elusive flavour like the smell of a dewy posy of wild flowers, fresh picked by fairy fingers from lush early morning pastures in which the scents, now meadow sweet and ferns seem to predominate in turn.*

I knew Morton Shand at the end of his life and I greatly respect his memory and his writings, but I must say that

127

when it comes to Steinwein in Bocksbeutel, and I have had very many, I cannot say more than that it is an extremely good wine. I hope, however, that you are curious enough to check him on it.

The origin of the Bocksbeutel itself is lost in antiquity and to quote Shand again:

It is a silly kind of bottle, difficult to ship, easy to break, it cannot be binned with any kind of facility, but it is a splendid vehicle for carrying the rather lush heraldic labels of Franconia.

It seems that any attempt to alter the shape of the bottle has been bitterly fought and indeed defeated by the local growers. Well, it may be truly said that there is good wine even in a bad bottle.

SEKT AND SPARKLING WINE

There is no special district, like Champagne in France, in which the whole of the grapes are used for making sparkling wine. Under the 1920 Peace Treaty, the Germans were forbidden by law to call their sparkling wine Champagne and they have never done so, but along the length of the Rhine there are very good wine firms who make brands of sparkling wine which is called *Sekt*, from more or less selected wine, and some of which is made by the *méthode champenoise*. In point of fact, researchers have found that the Germans were making sparkling wine before Dom Pérignon in Champagne, and this has developed in Germany over the centuries into quite a major industry. Sekt is made by two methods, by the *méthode champenoise* and in the case of the much cheaper *schaumwein* by vat storage, and sometimes impregnation of carbonic acid. All these cheaper wines, whatever the label may say, should be avoided, for they are neither good to drink nor interesting in any way. The label is often pretentious (and this, of course, is true in France too), but the contents are not amazing. The true Sekt, however, will if served properly, reach a very high standard and, while it is not Champagne, it has a good deal of character of its own. There are many well-known brands, and among the best are:

Deinhard & Co.	Kupferberg	Schönberger
Heinckel	Matheus Müller	Sohnlein

The Germans are a bit touchy about their Sekt and I well remember being entertained by a shipper in Worms who, not content with having proved exclusively the superiority of Liebfrauenstift and other fine German wines, went on to open bottle after a bottle of Sekt in the hope that I would say it was better than Champagne. It was an interesting party, and if it was not Champagne it was quite a good drink.

GERMAN WINE GLASSES

The normal, long-stemmed Hock glass is excellent, provided the bowl is of clear glass, for it is a great mistake to drink, as some people do, a fine wine or any wine out of glasses with coloured bowls. Good wine served in good condition is lovely to look at, lovely to smell, lovely to see, lovely to taste, and to use yet another of our senses, what could be more pleasant to the ear than the popping of the cork and the gurgle of the wine as it pours into the glass. Consequently, only clear white glasses should be used, although I may say I am attracted by the long green or yellow stems of the traditional German Moselle or Hock glass. Some of the older ones are pretty too, with their stumpy, knobby stems, but the bowl must be clear and white.

FAMOUS YEARS FOR GERMAN WINES

The miracle year for German wine was 1921, which was so good and so great that even today the wine, although dark, is still remarkable. I opened my last bottle only last year and it was splendid. The Hocks last longer than the Moselles, which are definitely lighter, and probably the Franconian wines last longest of all. But it is wise, generally, to drink German wine when it is reasonably young and certainly never more than ten years old, especially wine of no particular status. Obviously, the heavy wine, the *beerenauslese* or the *spaetlese*, will last longer, but you will be wise to drink them up fairly quickly. After 1921, there was a very good wine made in 1929; '34 and '35, particularly the last, were extremely good years, and '37. I don't know very much about the war years, but '45 was again good, and 1953 was the best post-war wine until the famous '59, which was superb and has been followed by good vintages in 1961, '62, '64 and '69.

5. THE WINES OF SPAIN

To most people, Spain is synonymous with sherry, that lovely wine which comes from Jerez de la Frontera near Seville in Andalusia, but this is by no means the end of the story. It is perfectly true, I imagine, that sherry is by far the biggest Spanish export, but many honest and sound wines are produced within the peninsula and have been ever since vines were planted in the long lost past, probably before the Romans. However, since sherry is the wine most of us associate with Spain, I will start with that delectable subject.

SHERRY

Sherry is a blend and never the wine of a single vineyard or a single year, and the wealth of Jerez is contained in the great *bodegas* which shelter butts of sherry and which are used for blending and which, collectively, are called '*soleras*'. The system of viticulture in this arid country where rain may not fall for many months is as follows: a hole is dug in the soil 8 feet or 9 feet down; it is filled with loose soil and the vine is planted in it. The object of this is to enable the original hole, which goes right through the clayey chalk, to form a pocket in which water from the winter rains can be stored in the loose soil, and indeed, the roots of the vine are some-times found to go down 10–15 feet. The vine grows, and in a few years grapes appear and are gathered from them, and according to the wine which is to be made from them, are left in the sun for a shorter or longer period to ripen or become over-ripe before being pressed. When I was last in Jerez in 1956 or '57, I saw the grapes being trodden by men wearing *zapatos*, the ironshod wooden boots, although perhaps by now more modern methods have come into use. The wine is fermented in the butt and long rows of these butts may be seen outside the vineyard, bubbling and fizzing away. When the boisterous fermentation has died down, the wine is moved in the butt by ox-cart to the *bodega* of the firm by whom it has been bought, possibly Gonzalez Byass or Williams & Humbert or by La Riva, Harveys, or any one of the great firms in Jerez, and in the *bodega* it is sorted into the class of wine for which it is most suitable. For instance, the wine from the Macharnudo vineyard is most suitable for making *finos*, and the richer grapes from the soil of Guadaloupe make the darker wines, the Amontillados and the Olorosas.

Now because sherry is a drink which people like to have regularly, it must be of a consistent taste and quality and this, obviously, as in the case of tea and other things like it, even whisky perhaps, needs very skilful blending, so the great butts containing 108 gallons are put into racks or *soleras* in the vast cathedral-like *bodegas* and they are, from time to time, tasted and when they are fit and ready, they are blended with other, sometimes very, very old wines and from them come the brands and blends that you and I know, ask for and expect to get, the Tio Pepe of Gonzalez, the Walnut Brown of Williams & Humbert, or the Tres Palmas of La Riva, or the Bristol Milk of Avery, or the Bristol Cream of Harvey.

The basis of this is the *solera* system, an 'organization' of several (sometimes hundreds) butts of sherry of consistent quality, but different ages arranged in tiers in the *bodega* and from which wine is taken for blending, the butt being 'refreshed' with wine from a younger butt, thus ensuring a lively wine with some character from the mature butt.

Generally, the youngest butts are on the top of a four- or five-tier *solera* with the oldest at the bottom, but the wine of one butt is never entirely the original wine – all have been refreshed. According to the quality, 'refreshing' takes place more or less frequently. I know of one *solera* of only three butts and from the lowest butt, started in 1770, the equivalent of two dozen bottles, or 4 per cent, is taken every two years, and it is refreshed from a butt started in 1819, again refreshed from a butt started in 1890, which is refreshed from the finest and oldest Amontillado available.

Blending is an extremely skilful process and something that is a very remarkable experience to see – the blender with his tiny silver thimble-like cup on the end of a long cane, called a *valence*, dipping it into the middle of the barrel through the bung-hole and bringing out a sample from the middle of it, pouring it instantly and at arm's length into a glass (the cane is about 3 feet long and the glass is held in one hand and the cane in the other), tasting it, sniffing it and giving his orders to blend it with such and such a number butt from such and such a rack.

Because of the prolonged sun drying of the grapes, the sherry wine when first made develops considerable alcoholic strength almost at once, possibly up to 14° or 15° and the *finos* that are sold in Spain are not fortified in any way – they are sold as pure sherries and they are extremely light and delicate. For export, however, fermentation is stopped fairly early in the proceedings by the addition of brandy made from Spanish wine, which not only stops further fermentation but adds considerable strength to the sherry, and that is why the import duty of sherry is so much higher than it is for the natural wines, coming in as it does under the Customs' schedule for wine 'not exceeding 27°'.

Sherry varies greatly in price according to the quality of

the grape used and the age of the wines used for blending and, indeed, its sweetness. They can be blended to sell at all prices and sweet sherries have a fair quantity of sugar added and, consequently, a poorer quality of grape. But good sherry is never cheap, as may be seen from any reputable wine merchant's list.

The principal types of sherry are as follows:

Fino

This is a pure sherry often made from grapes grown in the Macharnudo district, very, very pale and extremely dry, but not always delicate as it should be. A perfect example of a supremely delicate dry sherry is La Riva Tres Palmas. These natural *finos* do not keep long once the bottle is opened and should always be served chilled.

Amontillados

These keep for many years; they are dark in colour; they can be quite dry and often are, and are suitable for drinking with soup, or at 11 o'clock in the morning with a biscuit.

Olorosas

These are heavy, fruity wines, much sweeter than the Amontillados and usually made from quite old *soleras*, something like a Madeira.

Manzanilla

This is the wine of San Lucca de Barrameda. It is made near the fishing village of that name, near the mouth of the Guadalquivir River. It is delicious, light sherry, with a faintly nutty flavour and I personally think it one of the most delicious.

Montilla and Moriles

These are types of sherry made near Cordoba, much farther to the east and much to be recommended.

Pedro Ximenez

This is the rich dessert wine of Jerez – over-sweet to most tastes, and in a very old *solera* it has something of the consistency of lubricating oil.

Jerez de la Frontera is not the only sherry town, although it is by far the most important one. There are also large *bodegas* in Puerto Santa Maria, just across the bay from Cadiz but, of course, Puerto Santa Maria draws most of its supplies from the country around Jerez. The Cordova sherry industry, Montilla-Moriles, produces very good wine, and I still have in my cellar a last bottle of 1875 Montilla, bought from a country house sale and authenticated at that date, which is still bone dry and very drinkable. A year or two ago the Spanish authorities decided that sherry could only be sold under that name if it came from the Jerez district. This ruled Montilla out of the picture, which caused some hardship. It is true that a great many of the larger sherry shippers used to buy Montilla, blend it with their own and sell it as sherry – and it was none the worse for it.

Sherry is never sold under the date of its making and although I have tasted one of a great year from the private cellar of a sherry shipper in Jerez, these wines are never sold for public consumption, neither, it must be admitted, are they any better. Consequently, there is no point in giving any vintage years, and indeed all summers are the same in the south of Spain – extremely hot.

MALAGA

Malaga at one time was extremely popular as the 'port' wine of Spain, and indeed it is made in much the same way. It has now gone out of favour these many generations and I should think it would be hard to find a vintage Malaga on a wine list today, although a good deal of it is imported and sold under the heading of port type. It is made in much the same way as port and has considerable character and staying power. It has not the special distinction of port wine, but it is by no means to be despised and I am glad to say that I still have a bottle of Malaga which is pre-1850 from the same country house sale as my Montilla. I had five bottles in all, and the first four were very good indeed.

TARRAGONA

Tarragona wine was much beloved in this country in the early part of the century and in the early '20s as a big, full, fruity and extremely cheap wine that could be bought in large flagons for very few shillings – I seem to remember less than two! It is a little over-sweet, red wine, by our standards today and it used to be sold in public houses for a few pence a large dock glass and was considered to be rather violent in its effects. I have drunk Tarragona with a certain amount of pleasure in and near Tarragona I must admit, and I believe that a great deal of it is still imported into this country and sold as an anonymous wine. It is certainly quite a drink, but not, I think, much else.

VAL DE PEÑAS

The wines of Val de Peñas, both red and white, are fruity, dull and not at all bad, especially in Spain. Some years ago, one could buy it over here, and I expect one still can, for very little, and it is most excellent value, provided one does not expect delicacy, which you are hardly likely to get anywhere else at that price. In Spain itself it can be bought in the wine shops anywhere between Madrid and the Mediterranean coast (Val de Peñas is made about 100 miles

to the east of Madrid on the road to Granada) for a few pesetas
a bottle if you take your own bottle – and a litre at that.

RIOJA

The wines of the Rioja, which are produced north-east of
Madrid, are the finest red wines produced in Spain and
there are one or two quite fine wines of a claret type made
there, including the famous Marques de Rescal which comes
to the table in a rather beautiful wired bottle which does not
improve the taste of the wine at all, but looks very well.
Marques de Rescal is generally marketed under the year of
its birth, though I must confess that I have never seen much
difference in the various years, but on most Spanish wines
the neck label is worth little and much to be distrusted. One
should classify the wine simply as old, moderately old and
young. It grows old with grace, but doesn't really improve
very much.

Nevertheless it must be agreed that the wines of Rioja
have a great deal in common with the finer French wines
mostly of the claret type, although the wines are made to
suit most palates. When the French vineyards were devastated by the phylloxera in the late '80s and '90s of the last
century, the French *vignerons* came to Spain, bought vineyards and made good wine and improved the viniculture in
order to make good wine to add to their very depleted
stocks of wine in Bordeaux. This tradition has been kept up,
and when later the French, having cured their own ills, left
Spain and let the phylloxera in, the know-how remained.
I think that the Rioja is one of the most beautiful wine-
growing districts in the world and travellers in Spain should
take the trouble to visit Haro and Logroño and see for themselves and taste some of the delicious wines which are made
in and near those delicious towns.

OTHER SPANISH WINES

Vines are grown throughout the whole of Spain with the exception of one or two provinces near the French border on the Atlantic coast, and generally they are natural wholesome wines upon which a magician has waved a magic and sugary wand. Vast quantities are made on the Mediterranean seaboard centred on Almeria, and this roughly corresponds with the Midi in France insofar as the wine is good, fruity and dull. Wines of the Basque country are heady and sharpish and can be delicious. They should not be kept in the boot of your car for very long because they are apt to explode. In Catalonia, that is to say Villafranca de Panades they make excellent wine, red, white and rosé. The red laced with the famous priorato wine which is probably the strongest natural wine in the world (and not at all nice to drink) is sometimes called bull's blood and tastes much better than it sounds. North of Barcelona there is also an excellent wine of some character made.

As is happening in the minor vineyards of France the *vignerons* of Spain are becoming up to date in their methods and producing altogether better wine than has ever been produced before, some of it is very good indeed.

THE SPANISH SPARKLING WINES

There are some made in Perelada, a fabulous feudal castle with a large vineyard attached, just west of the Costa Brava and some from the white wine made there, too. Sparkling Spanish wine, however, must no longer be called Spanish Champagne, as it will be remembered in the famous case in 1961 that the French Champagne Association proceeded against the Spaniards for selling their sparkling wine as Spanish Champagne and won the case, and from that time it has been prohibited by this legal ruling. Spanish sparkling wine at its worst is rather bad, over-sweet and not at all to our taste. But at its best, it can be quite drinkable. The best I have tasted is the *Ne plus ultra* of Cordonniu which is also at the back of the Costa Brava and which claims to have the biggest sparkling wine cellars in the world, although whether this be true or not I have no knowledge. They make many qualities of sparkling wine, most of them sweet and sickly to our taste, but the one I have mentioned is dry and very drinkable.

BRANDY

Vast quantities of brandy are produced in Spain and it is almost as cheap as wine in the wine shops. It doesn't compare with Cognac and I never met a Spaniard who considered that it did, which is something. It can be quite drinkable, especially some of the more reputable brands like Fundador and Hispano, but it lacks the finesse of Cognac. If dates are found on the neck labels of the bottles, any similarity with the date of the year in which it was made would be a very rare coincidence.

Spain is a wine-loving country and grapes are grown over most of its surface. French wines and other wines are hard to obtain and very expensive, and, in any case, there is simply no need to buy them for, with the possible exception of Champagne, the best of the domestic wines are perfectly good even for special occasions, if carefully selected.

6. THE WINES OF PORTUGAL AND MADEIRA

The name of port has long been synonymous with the rich, sweet after-dinner wine superlatively drinkable after dinner, but port is by no means the only wine produced in Portugal. There are many, indeed dozens, of very good table wines produced in Portugal, some from pre-phylloxera grapes, unknown elsewhere in Europe, but since port is so well known we will deal with it as a separate subject and with the other wines of Portugal afterwards.

PORT

All port has this in common – it is made from grapes grown on the upper reaches of the Douro River; it is made into wine and put into cask, then shipped down the river to Oporto where it is stored in the lodges of the great port shippers and merchants, and there it is dealt with according to its type, quality and age, and is exported in three different ways.

Firstly, and most famously, as *vintage* port; this is the port of a given very exceptional year blended from wine made from the grapes of that year and of such supreme quality that the shipper will declare the vintage and ship that wine, usually in bulk, under the year in which it is made and under his own name.

Secondly, as *ruby* ports, which are blends of ports of different years and with a rich red colour and which may be drunk at any time and will not improve greatly if left long in bottle, which is, of course, the chief attribute of vintage port. Ruby port can be sub-divided into clear port matured in cask until bottled for consumption which can be decanted at any time (most club ports are of this sort), or crusted port which, being laid down for a period in bottle, does in fact throw a crust like vintage port.

Thirdly, we have *white* or *tawny* ports which have most of the characteristics of port, but are light in colour, not white, which is a misnomer; they are light gold in colour and can be dry, but possess their own flavour, with no pretence to that of sherry or Madeira. White or tawny ports are great favourites in some parts of the world as apéritifs and, indeed, they may be drunk as such, rather like some Madeiras, although they are rather cloying to my taste.

Vintage Port

Let us deal first of all with the magic, and magic it surely is, of vintage port. The wine, as we have seen, is made in the *quintas* in the upper reaches of the Douro. The grapes are, even today, crushed by treading. At the right moment the boisterous fermentation is checked by running off the wine into vats or casks where the correct amount of brandy is waiting for it. This pure grape brandy is made from Portuguese wine and this will give to the wine the tremendous staying and lasting power of vintage port, although the same process is also used for the other types of port. Once the wine has been made, blended perhaps with the wine of other *quintas* and lodges of the same year, and marked with the name of the famous shipper as a vintage, it is left in cask and shipped to England and stays in cask (or *pipes* as they are called) containing about 55 dozen bottles; it is bottled about two years later in the case of a light vintage and three years normally after shipping. Thus will be seen on the wine lists terms like: Cockburns 1917 bottled 1920, or Sandemans

1927 bottled 1930, and sometimes in the case of the last vintage bottled 1929. The bottling date is largely a matter for the London end of the shippers who will choose that moment in time when the wine should be bottled, at its most perfect stage of development. Thereafter, the wine will lie in bin for as many years as the fortunate owner can keep off it. We have all seen vintage port bottles which are never labelled, with merely a dash of whitewash at the bottom end to show which way up they should lie, and since the bins in port cellars are usually dark they will show up in the faint light of a candle. Then for a few years, the port will lie, always in the same position, and crust will form and lie along the bottles. Crust is a living organism in port, an almost microscopic life form, which has its being, lives and dies and sinks to the bottom, rather like coral in the sea. Some time or other, vintage port will cease to throw off crust, and at that time it may be said to be dying, but it takes a very long time to die.

Most vintage ports, if they are properly made and shipped by a great house, will last for fifty years, but today they hardly ever get it. The great years of the last century are very venerable indeed and that is why great years of port stand out as milestones in the history of wine, the comet year of 1811, the marvellous 1847, which is still being drunk today if it can be found; I have been invited to look at a bottle in Liverpool and will surely make the journey. The trouble with port is that it does rot the cork, and that is why, in the days of our grandfathers, care was taken to recork the port at intervals of thirty years or so.

Nowadays, of course, few people can afford to lay down a pipe of port or indeed to lay down very much at all. It gets no cheaper and has largely gone out of favour for this reason, because really to appreciate port one needs to drink it fairly regularly. If you don't, it is, by reason of its special alcoholic quality, rather prone to give one a hangover the next morning, and this too, I think, has contributed to its decline in popularity. Nevertheless, port-drinking shows signs of coming back and a very good thing, too. It has been well said that drinking port after dinner brings out the best in everybody – good conversation, good humour, wit, and benevolence. This I firmly believe to be true.

In the days of our forefathers, port bottles held about a pint – that is to say, two-thirds the size of our present bottle, hence the reputed three-, four-, five- and even six-bottle men of the eighteenth century. I am not sure whether port was as heavy and strong as it is now, but since during the Napoleonic Wars it was largely drunk as a substitute for claret, I imagine not. Certainly, vast quantities were imported at that time, but our wine trade with Portugal started much earlier than that – long before: in fact 1703 when the Methuen Treaty was signed, one of the first trade treaties ever to be made between England and another country. Later on, of course, there have been other treaties between Portugal and ourselves and in one of them, I forget which, it was agreed that the British would enact a law whereby no wine other than that made in Portugal could be termed port, and this, with the exception of Champagne, is the only wine so protected in this year of grace.

A word must be said about the great port houses whose headquarters are in Oporto, and many of them have their London houses, too. When the Methuen Treaty was signed, a great many members of the British wine trade, largely Scotsmen, went to Portugal and founded their branches, and these houses are still in existence today, and indeed continue to flourish in spite of the decline in port. The great merchants' houses, or lodges, are to be found along the south bank of the Douro River at Oporto and these face, on the north bank, the greatest wine club in the world, the Factory House at Oporto, established in the seventeenth century, and which has become a shrine of port lovers all over the world ever since. Here you will find the visitors' book signed by the Duke of Wellington's officers during the Peninsular War, and in the cellars, some of the wine he drank at that time, although I doubt whether it will be given to you and me.

Here is a list of some of the great port shippers which are still household words in the wine world today, and many of them were in existence in the eighteenth century:

Canova & Co. Ltd.
Cockburn Smithes & Co. Ltd.
Croft & Co. Ltd.
Davis, Hammond & Barton Ltd.
Evans, Marshall & Co. Ltd.
Feuerheerd Wearne & Co. Ltd.
Percy Fox & Co. Ltd. (Warre's Port)
Gonzalez Byass & Co. Ltd.
Grierson, Oldham & Adams Ltd.
Hunt Roope & Co. Ltd.
C. Kinloch & Co. Ltd.
C. N. Kopke & Co. Ltd.
Mackenzie & Co. Ltd.
Martinez Gassiot & Co. Ltd.
Merritt Huthwaite & Co. Ltd.
Morgan Bros. (London) Ltd.
Offley Forrester (London) Ltd.
J. R. Parkington & Co. Ltd.
H. Parrot & Co. (London) Ltd.
Reid, Rye & Campbell (Graham's Port)

Rutherford, Osborne & Perkins Ltd. (Quinta do Noval)
Geo. G. Sandeman Sons & Co. Ltd.
Sarano & Co.
J. Serra & Sons Ltd.
Silva & Cosens (London) Ltd. (Dows' Port)
Smith Woodhouse & Co. Ltd.
Taylor, Fladgate & Yeatman (Taylor's Port)

It is on the judgement of the principals of these firms that vintage port is blended, made and shipped, and there have been odd vintages – 1911 was one of them, I think – when only two firms, Martinez and Sandemans, felt they could ship 1911 as a vintage, mainly because they happened to be in a district of the Douro where rain fell and they knew it would materially alter the quality of the crop, whereas in other parts of the Douro where rain did not fall the crop was not sufficiently good to declare a vintage. Thus it quite often happens, and the fact that Cockburns or Grahams or Warres or Fonseca (or indeed any good names) have declared a vintage is sufficient guarantee for you and me. We shall have the very best port.

England lost a great deal of port during the last war from bombing, and went six years without replacements, and there is but little left of pre-war vintages and certainly practically none which can be bought, however reputable your wine merchant may be. Every now and again, a lot will come up at Christies' of, say, '27 port which is probably the greatest vintage of the century so far, and still at the very peak of its delicious power, but it will cost a great deal of money. The best port years of this century, apart from '27 which was undoubtedly the best, were 1900 when all shippers except Dow and Graham shipped; 1904 which was splendid and of which I have many pleasant recollections;

1908 which, until the 1927s came into their full power, I always considered the finest port I had ever drunk; 1911 was only shipped by Martinez and Sandeman for the reasons I have given you and was very good indeed; the 1912s are excellent, and then we have to go to 1917 which was quality rather than quantity year and shipped by a number of houses; 1920 was a good year, or good enough at least for most of the houses to ship a vintage (only Cockburns and Martinez did not); 1922 was good, and also 1924; 1927 was a great year, and he is a very lucky man who is given '27 after his dinner; thereafter, 1935 was good, and 1942 and 1945, when port could not, of course, be shipped to this country, and it was bottled in Oporto and laid by for shipping to this country as and when shipping space became available, which was not until 1949 or '50. This was a great experiment, which seems to have come off.

'Ruby' and 'White' Ports

Ruby port is a wine you will most commonly drink and be given to drink because it is shipped by the same shippers and it is much less troublesome than vintage port and, of course, correspondingly less expensive. It is not necessary to keep it for anything up to twenty years before drinking it and it is indeed quite excellent wine. Most of the great shippers list it with your wine merchant and in more than one quality; you may pay your price and take your choice. As I have said earlier, in talking about the service of wine, I see no reason why you should not decant it and it will taste none the worse, and will look a lot better. Some ruby ports throw crust – this is another reason for fairly careful decanting.

Tawny or white port: the same remarks apply to these excellent wines as for ruby port above. They are skilful blends of very high standard and probably best drunk as the

French drink them, as apéritif wines, or with dessert, when they are delicious if brought to the table thoroughly chilled (with fruit salad or a peach they are quite delicious). They are what they are, and if I took another two pages to describe them thoroughly I would not really tell you much more about them; you must try them for yourself.

THE NATURAL WINES OF PORTUGAL

The table wines of Portugal – that is to say, those unfortified wines which cannot in any way be described as port, but are purely natural fermented wines, some of them of considerable character. They are not commonly available in this country except for one or two brands which are being shipped and widely advertised and which are becoming popular. Among these is the Mateus rosé wine which is sold in a flagon, rather like the German Bocksbeutel, with a very beautiful label. This wine, which is a lovely rose colour, is slightly *pétillant* – that is to say, it has a tendency to sparkle if it gets half a chance. It is slightly sweet, and like the German Liebfraumilch some think it is a good wine to order for a mixed dinner in a restaurant when some guests are eating chicken or fish, and others steak or red meat.

These following are the principal wine-producing districts of Portugal and the type of wine they produce, although few are available on the market here. All are good and would, I think, compete favourable with some of the minor French wines if they were available. They are honestly made and some have remarkable keeping qualities.

Setubal

This amber coloured, luscious wine is made from white and black *muscatel* grapes and it is said to get its fantastic flavour from the local technique of restoring some of the grape skins to the cask *after* fermentation has stopped, until the following spring. Setubal wine is extremely rich and very much a dessert wine.

Colares

Colares wines come from the hillsides of Cintra near Lisbon and the wines are made from grapes grown from what must be the only pre-phylloxera vines left in Europe, except a few in Setubal. The wine is made from the *ramisco* grape and was once called 'Colares Port', which fairly describes it: a sweetish clean wine which has an affinity with port before it becomes *Port* if you know what I mean! Not a wine for children.

Carcavelos

This is near to Lisbon and makes a straw-coloured, dry to medium wine with rather an attractive flavour – Morton Shand thought, of almonds. I can vouch for its lasting properties, having only last year drunk my last bottle of a small bin of 1845 – an incredible age for a white wine. Every bottle was drinkable, a little tired perhaps, but no more so than I shall be at half the age.

Bucelas

The *arinto* grape makes the wine of Bucelas, a wine town near Lisbon. It is an amber, soft wine, much in favour in early Victorian England before the Queen discovered Hochheim, and is said to have been ruined by disreputable wine merchants lacing it with bad brandy, but in its natural form it is an acceptable, clean wine and goes well with fish.

Torres Vedras

Most of the natural beverage wines of Portugal are grown in this area; they are rather like the French Midi wines, clean and rather uninspired.

Dão

The vineyards are terraced on the hillsides along the Rivers Dão and Mondego, shut away behind mountains, and making red and white wines of very good quality of a sweetish type.

Vinhos Verdes

Vinhos Verdes or green wines are made in the north of Portugal and are dryish wines, green in tint and meant to be drunk 'green' or young. They are fresh and clean in Portugal, but not easily found here.

MADEIRA

Madeira comes, as one might think, from Madeira, an island about the size of the Isle of Wight some 500 miles out in the Atlantic from the coast of Morocco, discovered by the Portuguese navigator Goncalves Zarco in 1419. At that time, the island was covered with forest. It did not take long for vines to be planted, but conditions were not very suitable at first and the vines were afflicted with every disease known to gods or men, and it was only after hardy American stocks were imported (as in the case of the French vines) that the vineyards flourished, as they still do.

Madeira can be very old indeed and, it seems, without detriment to the wine. It is normally made on the solera system (see Sherry above) but it has much greater lasting properties. Sherry, for instance, is normally not very good after a very few years in bottle, whereas it is quite possible to get the great Madeira soleras of 1789, 1795, 1846, 1908 and so on, which are all excellent. Rarer, of course, are the vintage Madeiras of which there are very few left, but when found, also have very remarkable keeping properties and, in fact, I suppose one could say that Madeira is the longest lived wine of any, including port.

Madeira, like port, can be used either for dessert wine or in its dry qualities, like Sercial, instead of sherry, before a meal and, of course, one is always hearing about a glass of Madeira and a biscuit with one's bank manager at 11 in the morning. I personally never had such an enlightened bank manager, or if I did I never knew it, for I did not come under the category of customers to whom bank managers give glasses of Madeira. Be that as it may, a glass of Bual Madeira with a dry biscuit at 11 o'clock is a very happy institution and I can recommend it.

Quite early on in the development of Madeira, Malvasia vines were brought in from Cyprus and make a very sweet, excellent Madeira, which is also called Malmsey and indeed, any Malmsey you drink now is practically certain to come from Madeira and not from Cyprus. Madeira as a wine is much to be recommended. It is delicious whether dry or sweet; it is agreeable to the palate and never harsh and it has a flavour of its own; it is also very agreeable to the stomach, or, at least, it is to mine. At the risk of offending my friends in Jerez, I may say I prefer Madeira to sherry in general.

7. THE WINES OF ITALY

The vine grows everywhere in sunny Italy and wherever the
vine grows wine is made, and very good wine it is. There are,
of course, places in Italy where rough wine is sold at a rough
price, but by and large one can drink good wine at a reasonable price anywhere. I have never quite understood why it
is fashionable to charge comparatively high prices for Italian
wine in this country; it ought not to be. Wine is cheap

151

enough in Italy and yet it is difficult to get a Chianti or Orvieto wine over here for much less than £1 a litre flask or *fiasco*, as it is called. The wine is worth it, certainly, but if it were cheaper I am sure a great deal more would be sold.

Most Italian wines are honest, for the sun shines strongly during the Italian summers and ripens the grapes well, and little sugar is needed, if any. Both red and white grapes flourish, and red and gold wines are traditional in their districts.

THE WINES OF TUSCANY

The best known wine of Italy in the English market is Chianti, the great wine of Tuscany, and grown at its very best in the hills around Arezzo, Florence and Pisa. The best Chianti is (according to legend) reputed to be made from a more or less secret formula and contains three different kinds of grapes, which is true, and also includes a certain herb, which may not be true. It is also said that unless this herb occurs in the district, good Chianti cannot be made. The *Chianti Classico*, made only in the districts of Arezzo, Pisa and Siena, has a distinguishing external sign of a black cockerel on the neck label, which is limited to wine produced in these districts. Chianti at its best, drunk, shall we say, in Pisa, Florence or Siena, is clean, heady and, in my view, quite delicious. It used mostly to come in the straw-covered *fiascos*, impossible to bin, and delightful to look at. The finest Chianti, however, is bottled and occasionally, in good years, it can be given a date, which is comparatively rare and not terribly important. People do not associate Chianti and Italian wines with any special keeping qualities, but I can vouch that they can keep for a very long while. I acquired some years ago a bin of Barone Ricasoli Chianti of 1921 which has become mellow with age, and in its fifty-first year has a breed and distinction which would not dishonour a good Médoc or Burgundy.

The noble wines of Montepulciano again are rich garnet coloured, all the better for a few years' keeping, when they develop a very good bouquet.

Brunello di Montalcino – dark red, rather dry wine of strong flavour.

Moscatello di Montalcino – this is an aromatic muscat wine, rather sweet to our taste and a good dessert wine, bright golden colour.

Montecarlo wines are both dry wines and excellent in their class, made from grapes on the hills of Valdinievole. The white wine is splendid with fish or eggs, and all the better for being a year or two in cask.

Vernaccia di S. Gimignano is made from *Vernaccia* grapes and comes from the mountain town of S. Gimignano with its myriad towers all trying to get higher than the others. An altogether unforgettable experience is to sit outside a café on an evening in May in the square of S. Gimignano with the towers all around and drink this velvety, straw-coloured wine.

There are two types of wine made in Elba: the white, light straw-coloured and rather strong bouquet and very clean wine of considerable character. The red wine is almost black in colour with strong bouquet, but rather sweet for red wine, and it is made at Aleatico.

Vino Santo Toscano is made in several parts of Tuscany from the over-ripe grapes; it is rather sweet, delicately perfumed and, with age, makes an excellent dessert wine.

UMBRIA

The famous white wine of Orvieto rivals the red Chiantis and it is perhaps the favourite wine of Rome, extremely well balanced and clean; it is best drunk in an open-air restaurant overlooking the hills, somewhere near the Villa Borghese.

LATIUM

The Wines of Castelli Romani

South-east of Rome near the Alban Hills are the Castelli Romani, the little hill towns at one time fortified, nestling amid not very high peaks and surrounded by their vineyards. My idea of heaven is to sit on a summer day on the terrace of the restaurant looking down on the perfect circle of Lake Nemi and drinking the local wine, probably made from grapes from the vineyard stretching down below the restaurant to the water's edge. I do not think the wines are exported and I doubt if they will travel, but delicious they are.

Malvasia di Grottaferrata is made from grapes grown on the hills around that place, and has a pleasant flavour.

I suppose everybody knows the story of Est! Est!! Est!!! of Montefiascone, but in case not, here it is. Bishop Fugger of Bavaria on a visit to Rome in AD 1111 sent his steward before him to mark the place where he should eat and where he should stay overnight, and particularly to note the inns with the best wine, and so the steward did, marking the inn of his choice with '*est*', that is, 'here is good wine' (*vinum bonum est*). And so all went well until the steward came to Montefiascone, and there the wine was so marvellous, he wrote in large characters, '*Est! Est!! Est!!!*' – 'It is! *It is!!* IT IS!!!' and so indeed it is a very excellent wine indeed, with a very high reputation to live up to which I am not quite sure it fully deserves. But don't make any mistake about it, it is excellent wine, rather sweet, because it is made from *muscat* grapes.

Aleatico del Viterbese is the red wine of the Gradoli

district, with purple bubbles winking at the brim, and it is in fact too sweet for English taste.

CAMPANIA

Wines of Falerno are famous for their keeping quality and the Roman poet Horace cried aloud, 'O for Falernian wine an hundred years old'. This is made just north of Naples in the fantastic district known as the Campi Flegrei, the Phlegian Field, and the districts of Formia and Mondragone. Deep ruby red in colour, it is very good wine indeed; strong and good. I have never tasted Falerno wine 'an hundred years old', but I would like to.

Lacrima Christi of Vesuvius comes to us both red and white; it is grown on the slopes of Vesuvius and the white is amber tinted, superlatively delicate and slightly aromatic, an extremely good wine with the superb fish of the district. The red wine from the eastern and southern slopes of Mount Vesuvius is brilliant red and smooth to the taste. There is an ordinary Vesuvius wine made on the south-east slopes with rather less alcoholic content and purplish in colour, but extremely pleasing.

The wine of Capri is yellow, straw coloured and very pleasant, but Capri is so beautiful that it would be difficult to find a bad wine.

Other Campania wines are made at Conca; Gragnano; Ravello (which is made red, white or rosé); Salopaca; Taurasi; Greco di Tufo.

VENETIA AND PIEDMONT

I suppose one of the most famous white wines of Italy is the Soave, the not too light wine made in the districts of Soave and Monteforte. This wine is sold in most of the northern Italian cities and is extremely well balanced, dry, flavoury and of light straw colour. Soave also makes a good dessert wine from over-ripe grapes, which is called Recioto. Bardolino wine is made from grapes growing in Bardolino and neighbouring territories on the south-east shore of Lake Garda, and it is a bright clear ruby red. Again it is dry, and indeed sometimes slightly tart, but fine, lively table wine.

Valpolicella is a full red wine with a characteristic bouquet, grown from grapes on the Valpolicella hills and best drunk when there.

Recioto Veronese is a sweet red wine with an attractive flavour and grown in the Valpolicella district. Only the over-ripe grapes on the outside of the bunches are used and the wine has an alcohol content of 13°. Sparkling wine is also made in this district.

Perhaps the best red wine in Italy is from Gattinara in Piedmont and this not only lives to a great age but is in a class by itself in the same way as a great château claret or domaine burgundy will stand up with its fellows. It is run pretty close by the Barbaresco and Barolo. All these wines when found – and it is hard to find them – undoctored can be absolutely marvellous. I have tasted Gattinara wines thirty years old which have shown no sign of age at all. These wines are made mostly from the Nebbiolo grape and as Michelin would say 'worth a considerable detour' to sample.

WINES OF EMILIA

Lambrusco di Sorbara made from the Lambrusco grape in vineyards in the province of Modena is brilliant red in colour and characteristic in flavour, but it can be sweetish and very fruity. It has a *pétillant* quality and foams at the brim. It is supposed to be good with fat foods, and it is appreciated by most people who like their wine a little on the sweet side.

Sangiovese di Romagna comes from the hills of Romagna; a light wine with a dry flavour and it has a reputation of keeping well.

Albana di Romagna is a deep golden yellow wine of the same district, very agreeable to those who like their wine a little sweeter than dry. It is velvety and altogether a pleasing wine. There is a sweeter quality which is suitable for dessert.

APULIA AND LUCANIA

Sansevero is a pale yellow wine which can be quite strong, with a dry velvety taste.

Martina Franca and Locorotondo from the hills of the Martina Franca, slightly greenish-straw coloured and dry flavoured, both make good table wines and are the basis for the local vermouth.

Castel del Monte can be either deep ruby red or rosé, rather fruity, but dry and smooth.

Other wines from Apulia and Lucania are Aleatico di Puglia, a light red wine with a tonic flavour, Moscado del Salento, or simply Salento, wine which is either white or red and extremely sweet; only really suitable for dessert wine. Squinzano, Barletta, Primitivi di Manduria e del Tarantino: these are heavy wines, but mainly used for blending with lighter ones. Aglianico del Vulture – garnet red in colour and a full round taste. Moscati di Lucania and Moscato di Trani are the sweet wines of these famous places and the Malvasia di Lucania and Malvasia di Brindisi are made from Malvasia grapes and can be got in two qualities, the dry which is made from the ordinary grapes and is generally excellent, and sweet which can have as much as 15° of alcohol, and is deep amber in colour, made from over-ripe selected grapes and excellent for people who like fairly sweet wines.

THE WINES OF CALABRIA

Travelling south through Italy, the wines tend to become more and more harsh, but there are some extremely good wines made on the foothills of the mountains. Among them, Savuto in the province of Cosenza, a dry velvety rich red wine, sometimes going up to 15° of alcohol, Cirò di Calabria from the districts of Cirò and Melissa of Catanzaro not far from the fabulous Cirò Massif, the Switzerland of Calabria. It can be had dry or sweet.

Greco di Gerace is from the province of Reggio Calabria and right in the toe of Italy. It has a fantastic alcoholic content of 17° and is bright amber yellow, it has a delicate bouquet, and is said to be redolent of orange blossom, which it could be. An excellent dessert wine.

Lacrima di Castrovillari comes from the province of Cosenza and is the red wine of the district, dry and pleasant.

Moscato di Cosenza is made from the yellow Muscat grape and is again heady, amber yellow, aromatic and much too sweet for me.

SICILY

Marsala, I suppose, is the best known wine of Sicily and is in fact made like port and Madeira, and it has very many of their virtues. Made on the *solera* system, it lasts to a very great age and I think it has more affinity with Madeira than port. Certainly, Marsalas last thirty, forty or fifty years.

The wines of Etna are very good indeed. The slopes of Etna are wonderfully fertile and rich and it seems to be the only justification for living on that very chancy mountain, as anybody who has travelled round it will know; nevertheless, it is the most thickly populated area in Sicily, the main reason being, of course, the high fertility of the soil. The Etna wines are made white or red and are generous, fruity and good. Rosé types are also produced.

Malvasia di Lipari is made from Malvasia grapes in the Ionian Islands between Salina and Stromboli, golden yellow in colour, but a rather sweet dessert wine.

Moscato di Pantelleria made from the Muscat grapes in the isle of Pantelleria is also bright amber and much too sweet for me, but an excellent wine for those who like it.

Mamertino from Messina province of Sicily is golden and dry with characteristic and strong bouquet. There is also a sweet quality made as a dessert wine.

Faro made in the hilly region about the Straits of Messina is bright red, rich and agreeable.

Eloro is made in both red and white categories, the red being slightly stronger than the white. Both are very good and not sweet.

Sicilian wines have the reputation of being unexpectedly heady, and indeed they are, and it is as well to look out after the first bottle.

Moscato di Siracusa and Moscato di Noto, made from muscat grapes, are, as may be expected, extremely sweet; they are rich wines with a pleasant bouquet.

The Frappato di Vittoria in the Province of Ragusa is cherry red, and again rather rich and sweet.

WINES OF SARDINIA

The Vernaccia di Sardegna from the lower Tirso Valley is a very strong wine indeed with up to 18° of alcohol; it is a bright amber colour with a velvety, strong flavour and claims to be one of the noblest white wines in the world. It is certainly an exceedingly interesting one.

Nuragos is heady, like most of these island wines, but dry and clean, with up to 15° of alcohol.

Nasco, golden yellow in colour, is rather sweet with a dry finish.

Monica di Sardegna, made from the monica grape, is purplish, mellow and very sweet.

Girò di Sardegna has very much the same characteristic as the Monica made from the Girò grape.

Oliena or the Nepente di Oliena, the favourite wine of the poet d'Annunzio, is a rich red wine with lovely bouquet and rather an odd after-taste.

Malvasia di Bosa in the Bosa hills is golden yellow in colour and best drunk a year or two old.

Vermentino di Gallura is straw coloured, dry and heady.

THE SPARKLING WINES OF ITALY

Sparkling wine or spumante (which means 'sparkling') is made in most Italian wine districts in small quantities, but the finest and best comes from Asti in Piedmont, and it was started in the second half of the nineteenth century when great French Champagnes were in their heyday. I have never heard that the Asti district is very much like the soil of Champagne, but then again, neither is the wine, and indeed they have only one thing in common: they both sparkle and for the same reason – carbonic acid gas. The Asti wines in their own particular way are extremely good and especially for those who like their wine sweeter rather than drier. There are, however, some good dry spumantes, but they must be sought after.

The best spumante is made in the same way as Champagne by the *méthode champenoise*, and in the cellars of the great Asti spumante manufacturers can be found literally millions of bottles maturing in the same way and under similar conditions as in the caves of Rheims or Epernay. Asti is the celebration drink of the Italians and is generally drunk throughout Italy in the same way that Champagne is throughout England and France, and it has also quite a faithful following in England from people who have got the habit from their visits to Italy.

Spumante is made from blends of grapes and not from the grapes of any special year or vineyard. There is red and white spumante and rather delicate rosé, and the following is a list of shippers who make very good wine in this country :

Felice Bonardi

Luigi Bosca & Figli

Canova Caligaris S.R.L.

Giuseppe Contratto S.p.A.

Cantine Bruno Ferrari S.p.A.

Fontanafredda Tenimenti di Barolo e Fontanafredda

Fratelli Gancia & C. S.p.A.

Figli di Marengo Antonio

Mirafiore – Vini Italiani S.A.

C. & L. Vallarino

Alessandro Zoppa

8. THE LITTLE WINES OF EUROPE
AND THE MEDITERRANEAN

There are many good and refreshing, if not great, wines grown within the continent of Europe.

This book is intended to be essentially practical – that is to say, since I would expect that people reading it would want, at some time or another, to drink the wines, there would not appear to be much point in devoting whole chapters to wines which cannot be drunk because they cannot be bought. Nevertheless, this would not be a hand-book if some of these wines were not specifically mentioned,

162

as well they deserve to be; the trouble is to know where to start. Many of the wines can hardly be termed 'little' in any sense. Since I must start somewhere, I will take a wine which is not sold often in England at all, but comes from a country well worth a visit.

LUXEMBURG

The grapes from which these wines are made are grown from vines on the low hills along the upper Moselle and they have a good deal of affinity with the German Moselle wines, although it is fair to say that they are not so carefully made nor is there a tradition of making great wines, as in Germany. Nevertheless, very large quantities of very good wine are made, mostly from the *Riesling* grapes, and if you ever go to the delightful Duchy of Luxemburg you will have ample opportunity of trying the wine. The vineyards start where the German vineyards end, at Wasserbillig on the frontier, and go on through Grevenmacher, Ahn, Wellenstein, and Remerschen. Quite wisely, the Luxemburgians drink their own wine and don't bother to import very much.

As far as I know, all the wine is white, and I don't remember having tasted any Luxemburg wine of really superb quality. On the other hand, they make a wine which is found hardly anywhere else and this is the Luxemburg *perlé*, which is a semi-sparkling or *pétillant* wine of considerable liveliness and charm. One can now buy it in England from Grants of Idol Lane (not St James's). I invariably order it as an apéritif if it is available. It is not that it is as good as Champagne (which is, of course, the perfect apéritif); it most certainly is not, but it is quite cheap, very clean and altogether excellent.

THE IRON CURTAIN AND COMMUNIST COUNTRIES

It is perhaps fortunate for us that, owing to the necessity of obtaining foreign currency, the wine-making Soviets or countries behind the Iron Curtain have exported a fair amount of good wine, which is sold at very reasonable prices.

Yugoslavia

Chief among these is the wine of Yugoslavia which you might be surprised to hear is now the twelfth largest wine-producing country in the world, according to Mr. T. A. Layton's book *Wine Craft* (Harper & Co. 1958). I have found the Yugoslav wines universally good; those drunk in Yugoslavia itself are rather dull, but certainly the export white wines are not only cheap but of some distinction. These wines are often exported in bottle and for what they cost here are extremely good value, comparing favourably with the wines of any other country at that price.

There is quite an important wine-making tradition in Yugoslavia which embraces the old kingdoms of Serbia and Montenegro.

Mr Penning-Rowsell (*Country Life*, 17th May 1961) has travelled extensively in Yugoslavia and has a very high opinion of the wine, and I am surprised to learn from him that the quantity of wine imported from Yugoslavia in 1960 was 225,000 gallons, about a third of the amount of wine imported from Germany. I am not sure what this signifies except that the wine is extremely good value (which it most certainly is), but whether the foreign exchange situation in this Communist country operates in our favour with regard to the price, I don't know. If it does, we ought to take advantage of it because the wine is, as I have said, clean and mostly dry.

Ljutomer and Maribor are the chief wine centres of Yugoslavia, but a good deal of wine is grown all along the Adriatic coast. The *Riesling* grape is the one in general cultivation, but, indeed, wine is made from quite a number of different breeds of grape and in various degrees of sweetness. Penning-Rowsell also says that the *pinot* grape, that is the Champagne grape, does not prosper although efforts have been made to improve the wine with it.

Hungarian Wines

We get very few Hungarian wines in England today, but there is a good deal of good white wine made in that country and at one time it was extremely popular over here. At Carlowitz in Serbia, they make a rich golden wine which became extremely popular in court circles in the middle of the last century, and I have in my possession a pair of decanters holding three bottles each, sandblasted with the inscription, 'Finest Carlowitz by Royal Appointment to Her Majesty Queen Victoria'. According to André Simon's encyclopedia of wine, this Hungarian wine attained a fair measure of popularity in England during the '60s; it is grown on the right bank of the Danube, thirty miles north of Belgrade. When I acquired the decanters they were, alas, empty, and I had never tasted that wine, but it must have been good to achieve such distinction.

I suppose that, most of all, Hungary is synonymous with Tokay which has always been another word for richness, fatness and good living. Above Tokay is, of course, the *Imperial* Tokay, and even above the Imperial Tokay, or perhaps because of it, the world-famous Tokay Essence or *Essenz*. Edmund Penning-Rowsell on a recent visit was given half a litre of this fantastic wine, which is still made and rarely sold and used for 'flavouring' fine wines, and through his courtesy I have been privileged to drink a glass.

It is a superlative wine, not so sweet as one would perhaps imagine, but of tremendous strength and character. At a recent sale at Christie's three half-litre bottles of this wine (admittedly nineteenth-century) fetched over £80 or $200 a bottle.

No book on wine would be complete without at least a few words about the almost fabulous Tokay, which is made in a strictly limited area and the wine varies from dry to very, very sweet indeed, and in some ways conforms to the German pattern of wine-making, from the ordinary wine made from ordinary grapes to the great *Trockenbeeren* vintages which are pressed and made from hand-picked over-ripe grapes, wrinkled and fat with sugar and covered in the *pourriture noble* of the *semillon* grape in Bordeaux. In the great days of Imperial Tokay, they went even further than this: the grapes were left so long that they were sometimes gathered in the snow in late November; then heaped in the vat so that the pressure of the grapes above broke the skins of those at the bottom and the viscous liquid which emerged was carefully collected and made into the very few bottles of the fabulous *Essenz*. It is reputed that from many acres of grapes of the finest quality, very few bottles would be made, and it had a high reputation for keeping millionaires alive as a more pleasant substitute for oxygen. According to Morton Shand, the wine is not of a high alcoholic content, merely 7° or 8°, but is reputed to have a fantastic delicate sweetness and takes years and years to mature. It has a reputation (perhaps with some reason) of having aphrodisiac qualities and Shand quotes a Dr Robert Drewett, MRCP, sometime medical adviser of health for the Parish of St George's, Hanover Square, who, in a lecture, said of Tokay: *Nor need I mince matters and refrain from saying that 'when childless families despair', when January is wedded to May, and when old men wish to be young again, then Tokay is in request. It was, I am told, a favourite drink of the Court of King George IV.*

Tokay, Imperial or otherwise, was and is made according to strength, and the gauge of this is called a *puttony*, which is the name of the vessel used for gathering the *Trocken-beeren* grapes, although the grapes are not necessarily rotten or over-ripe. The same measure is used in the classification of the wine in the bottle, thus you will see on the label Tokay, '3 puttonys', which means that it is a medium kind of wine and not over-sweet. The maximum is the '5 puttonys' which is a very thick, sweet wine, and if it is Imperial Tokay, next to the *Essenz*. 'One puttony' is quite a dry wine and is made like all Tokays from the *formint* grape.

There doesn't appear to be much point in writing a lot about Iron Curtain wines, apart from Tokay, and in any case the same remarks apply – the wines are well made from the *Riesling* grape and the common wines are clean and dry. Red wines are made, but not to the extent of white, and, in particular, there is an almost black wine called Bikaver which means 'bull's blood' and is made in the Egri district. This is a sound big wine and it can be bought in England.

Czechoslovakia

Few Czechoslovak wines are imported into this country or have been for some years, and I am again indebted to Edmund Penning-Rowsell, who has recently returned from Czechoslovakia, for the information that the wine yield exceeds that of Switzerland and that Czechoslovak domestic consumption by far exceeds supply; consequently it is extremely unlikely that we shall see any of it here for some years to come, but if you go to Prague or tour in that delightful country, you can expect to drink both red and white wines, and they are soundly made, honest wines. The white wines are better than the red.

Roumania

A surprisingly large amount of the world's wine is made in Roumania – it may be as much as 100 million gallons a year, mostly white. Very drinkable wines are made at Dragashani, Sarica, Constanza, Silistria, Delal Marc, Satul Marc, Tarnavale and Alba Julia. They are all made for general consumption.

The Crimea and Bessarabia

Russian wines may be bought in England, and these export wines are usually sound, low-priced, rather fruity wines with their own peculiar flavour, the appreciation of which might be termed an acquired taste. The sweet wines can be over-sweet, but some of the red *ordinaires* are good enough and will come either from the Crimea or from Akkerman in Bessarabia, or perhaps a blending of the two types. The sweet wines may be made from either *muscatel* grapes or perhaps the Spanish *Pedro Ximenez* grape, from which the very, very sweet sherries are made. So-called 'Russian Champagne' is made in considerable quantities in the Crimea, but it is, again, over-sweet and would (for me) take a century or two to acquire any taste for it.

SWITZERLAND

The wines of Switzerland are essentially for the Swiss as they hardly produce enough for their own consumption, and since Switzerland is an extremely lovely country, we may think it worth while to drink a few Swiss wines when we go there, or on our way through Switzerland to sunny Italy. I would particularly recommend the wines of the

Vallais, that long fruitful valley between the Lake of Geneva and Brig, en route for the Simplon Tunnel. All along this valley very good wine is made and it is well worth stopping for a little *dégustation* in the morning, or indeed at any time.

Probably the most famous Swiss wine comes from Neu-châtel, and these wines can indeed be found in one or two good restaurants in London, notably those where the managing director is Swiss. They are extremely good wines with something of an affinity with the Hermitages along the lower Rhône, but, alas, they neither keep nor travel and must be drunk within three or four years, and unless imported in bottle they will not be nearly so good as in their own country.

Both red and white wines are made in Switzerland and most of the red wines come from round Lake Constance and the southern part of Switzerland, and of course they have a good deal in common with the south German red wines. Quite frankly, they are not much, and the white wines do not compare with the best of Neuchâtel and other white wines made in Switzerland.

THE WINES OF MALTA

Vines have been grown and wine made in Malta since the Romans, but until recently the production has only been sufficient for domestic consumption within the island. A few years ago I visited Malta for a few days and I was able to study the wines at first hand, and I had the advantage of being taken around the wineries by Dr Perraulta of the Maltese Ministry of Agriculture.

This tiny island, with its even smaller sister island of Gozo, is rocky, stony, and sandy, and if poorness of soil is a qualification for making good wine Malta certainly ought to make it, and so it does. The wines have a strong affinity with the Italian wines and quite a lot of the expertise which is used in the making, blending and storage of the wines, comes from Northern Italy. Grapes are grown in small-holdings and very small holdings too, all over both islands, and they are sold to wineries established in three or four places, but mostly in the suburbs of Valletta. Great progress is being made in the betterment of the wine under govern-mental encouragement. Until recently, wines were made to be consumed in the year after the vintage – that is, quite new; they were for local consumption and varied in quality from very rough to moderately good, but there are now some excellent wines turned out and Malta is beginning to export quite a lot, largely in bulk, and I fear, as in most cases, it is used to assist the under-produced countries to close the gap between the supply and demand. This is a pity, because Maltese wine in its export quality is stable, extremely clean, palatable, rather light and very good beverage wine. No fine wines are produced, let alone great, but perhaps this will come, because the soil is right, and certainly there is plenty of sun to ripen the grapes. It remains to be seen whether the wine will keep for very long, but I have put a few bottles in my cellar to keep for a year or two to try this out.

THE WINES OF GREECE

Greek wine has been made longer than recorded history, for since the days of pre-classical Greece, the wine cup has always been a decorative motif on the sherds and pottery, of which there are so many lovely specimens in existence. Decorations, were, of course, used largely on wine cups and kraters (wine-mixing jars) of classical Greece and H. Warner Allen in his *History of Wine* (Cassell, 1961) gives an excellent

account of wine-drinking in ancient Greece and some of the
parlour games they played with the wine and wine cup.
Modern Greek wines are becoming quite well known over
here, and these are strong, heady beverage wines tinctured
with resin, and have a certain appeal for people who like a
distinctive, tasty drink. This flavoury wine isn't to everybody's taste, and certainly does not go well with any kind
of delicate food. The truth is, of course, that Greek wine is
made (as it should be) to suit the climate and the food of the
country, and the rather oily, greasy cuisine of Greece is
very suited to the heady resinous wines of the country.
Personally, I have no great objection to it in Greece, in fact,
I rather like it, and in Greek restaurants in London where it
is served in the best qualities; but heaven preserve you and
me from some of the native Greek wines which fortunately
are not exported here except for use in the manufacture of
British vermouth and other concoctions. The addition of
1–3 per cent of resin or turpentine to the young wine in
Greece has gone on from time immemorial and it is said that
this admixture helps to preserve the wine and renders it
more wholesome – a sentiment rather than an idea, I fear,
which I find hard to believe. Fortunately, however, modern
Greek practice tends to produce wines with and without
resin, but the resinous wines are nearly always served
unless the non-resinous wine is asked for.

The vine is grown all over Greece and the islands, and
some of the best wine I have tasted comes from Mount
Hymettus near Athens. It is made in red, white, rosé, dry
and sweet, and before condemning it out of hand from my
rather unenthusiastic description, you should try it for
yourself. It has a distinctive flavour and at its best is quite
drinkable – I suggest perhaps with Irish stew. Nevertheless,
if you are ever (and I hope you will be!) persuaded to visit

Greece, you have a great treat in store: to visit a *taverna*, enter through the kitchen, choose a dish or dishes from one of the dozen or so cooking on the stove, and sit down to it (or them) with a carafe of ice-cold Greek wine. Long may you survive!

THE WINES OF CRETE AND CYPRUS

Cyprus and Crete both grow vines and make wines both red and white which have, of course, a considerable affinity with Greek wines, and are plus and minus these wines according to taste. Cyprus may well be the origin of that butt of Malmsey wine, so beloved of historians, in which the infamous Duke of Clarence was supposed to have been drowned in 1478. (This like the story may not be true because Malmsey is made from the *malvoisie* grape in the Canaries and Madeira, but not, probably in 1478.) This feat must have been slightly difficult to achieve, unless the unfortunate Duke of Clarence was cut up into small pieces first, and pushed in through the bung-hole (when he would scarcely have been drowned), for wine then, as now, only emerges from the bung-hole of the barrel. He may well have been drowned in a water butt which once contained Malmsey, but hardly in the wine itself. As I have said, Malmsey is made from the *malvasia* (or *malvoisie*) grape; it is a sweetish wine and I do not remember seeing it in the current wine merchant's list, neither do I ever remember having been given it to drink in this country except as Madeira.

Apart from Malmsey, one must accept Cypriot and Cretan wines in a spirit of adventure – you may be delighted or you may be disappointed, or you may think they are good strong wines which suit your taste in food. Who knows?

TURKEY

The odd thing about the wines of Turkey is that I cannot find any reference to them in the older books of my gastronomic library. Although Turkey holds fifth place among the grape-growing countries of the world it holds one of the lowest places among the wine-producing countries, because most of the grapes are either sold as raisins, currants and sultanas, and for table grapes, or used for making grape syrup. According to André L. Simon, it was not always so and at the beginning of the century, Turkey produced as much as 15 million gallons of wine a year, 80 per cent for export.

Every kind of wine is made, but more white than red and some of it is quite heady, with an alcoholic content of up to 13.5°. Considerable effort is being made to improve the quality of the wines, a few of which are available in England. Tekirdag is a white wine, or rather a golden wine, not unlike a good Entre Deux Mers and up to the standard of other wines sold at the same price, which is about 40p a bottle.

EGYPT

Modern Egyptian wines, which are only bought in Egypt (thank God!), are made in the delta near Alexandria, and rumour says that they are made from raisins rather than grapes which, from the taste, is quite possible. They are dull wines with nothing much to commend them, least of all the price, which is high, but they have lovely names – Clos de Cléopatre and Cru des Pyramides among them. They are not much to our taste, as you will have gathered, but in a Moslem country wines are not very popular and viticulture lacks encouragement. Mohammed was against it and he says in the Koran, 'There is a devil in every berry of the grape'.

Historically, of course, records of wine and wine-making are the earliest extant and from the first dynasty, about 3000 BC onwards, there is constant reference in tomb-carvings and paintings to the place of wine in Egyptian life. As I have already mentioned in my Introduction, an interesting fact not generally known is that the most definite proof of the number of years which the young King Tutankhamen (of Lord Carnarvon and Howard Carter fame) reigned was from the seals of the wine jars buried with him with his fabulous treasure in the unplundered tomb, found in 1922. Tutankhamen died in or about the year 1352 BC and the wine jars bear the royal seal, stating that the wine was made in the royal vineyards in the delta in the ninth year of his reign, and since wine in the East is always drunk very shortly after it is made, it can be reasonably assumed that the wine in the King's tomb would be that of the last vintage, and thus we know how long this young king reigned. The jars were sealed but, alas! no wine remained, only a desiccated powder. There is an apocryphal story of archaeologists finding in a royal tomb, which had been plundered like all the others of its treasure, two *amphorae* or wine jars lying in the corner, and these had been opened and the wine drunk by the robbers (most of the tombs were plundered in deep antiquity). Upon one of the *amphorae* the robber had scratched: 'This one contains the best wine.'

What the wine was like in those days we cannot know, but teetotal Islam has certainly not done any good at all to the modern Egyptian wine industry.

9. THE WINES OF SOUTH AFRICA, AUSTRALIA, NORTH AND SOUTH AMERICA

SOUTH AFRICA

Wines have been made from grapes grown in South Africa since 1655 or, I suppose, 1658, since we must assume that if the first vines were planted in 1655, we should allow them three years to give forth some fruit. The first vines were planted by Jan Van Riebeeck, the founder of Cape Colony, and he soon found that the soil was good and the vines prospered and that the wine was, I have no doubt, excellent. After Van Riebeeck came Simon van der Stel, who is known as the second founder of Cape Colony, and he was, or so his reputation says, extremely fond of good living. He built a very lovely farm, which is now one of the historic monuments of Cape Colony, at Groot Constantia, and here he made the best wine in the Colony and Constantia soon became famous for its wine. Constantia lies a little to the south of Cape Town, but the great vineyards of South Africa stretch along the Paarl Valley and the Little Karroo beyond the Drakensberg Range to the Swartberg Mountains, which are rather high in altitude. Here lie the famous wine towns and districts of Worcester, Robertson, Nuy and Barrydale, and here are made some excellent wines which I will not insult by calling them the names all too often seen on their labels: Hocks, Burgundies and so on. I prefer to call them, whatever the labels may say, Paarl wines or Worcester wines or South African white wines, or what have you,

175

because they have plenty to commend them without taking names of other places and claiming a character which they do not in fact possess.

Constantia wines soon became famous and Cape wine generally was popular in this country. I have had Cape wine of 1830 vintage (and still have a bottle) and very excellent it is, of a port type, so I assume the particular hogshead from which my wine has been bottled had been fortified. The wine came from the Ashburnham sale in Sussex and is bottled in eighteenth-century pint bottles. Over the bin was the porcelain label with CAPE 1830 upon it, and the name of the supplier, 'Mr Frisby'. I don't know who Mr Frisby was, but he had good taste in wine and could pick one which would last – 140 years at the moment. From this it can be seen that good wine has been made in South Africa because bad wine doesn't keep.

I suppose one of the most important, and certainly the best of South African export wines, is 'sherry'. I have to put 'sherry' in inverted commas because it does not come from Jerez in Spain, from whence comes the only wine really entitled to the name, but I would not know otherwise what to call this South African sherry because it is so similar in type, and I cannot really see what can be done about it, except to call it firmly South African sherry. Some of it, or perhaps one should say, most of it, is very, very good, especially of the dry types; it is made on the same *solera* system and tremendous care is paid to the blending and styling of different qualities. Cheap South African sherry is not very good, but then, neither is cheap anything.

The headquarters of the Co-operative Wine Growers' Association of South Africa (K.W.V.) is at Paarl, where they have an old Dutch house with a lovely ornamented gable roof which would do credit to the Herengracht in Amsterdam, and from this house is controlled, or at least, co-ordinated, the efforts of thousands of *vignerons* or growers in South African wine-growing districts. Paarl, Montagu, Worcester, Robertson and Stellenbosch have cellars with a capacity of nearly 50 million gallons of wine.

I do not personally care for the red wines as much as the white – it is dull by comparison, but the white are generally excellent. South African sparkling wine is much too sweet for my taste, and has an affinity with Italian Spumante. There are some good South African brandies, very good in fact, of the three star and below variety, but I do not believe that any really fine brandy can come out of South Africa – at least I have never tasted any.

I am not sure how to advise the intelligent reader to buy South African wines, and suggest a chat with his wine merchant, who will certainly be able to provide a few sample bottles for him to taste ('look at' is the delightful wine trade expression). The main thing is to 'look at' them and judge for yourself; you may well have a pleasant surprise.

AUSTRALIA

When Sir Philip Sydney took the first fleet to Australia in 1788, he included in his fantastic inventory of equipment, plants and seeds for the first settlers a few varieties of vines from France and Germany, and within three years he saw that the soil and the climate were suitable for the vine and reported accordingly. It was not, however, until James Busby, born in Edinburgh in 1801, emigrated to Australia that the industry, as we now know it, was started. Busby had studied viticulture before emigrating, and he returned to England and enlisted government support to make a tour of the wine-growing countries of Europe in order to develop the vine-growing and wine-making in what is now New

South Wales. Upon his return with something like 20,000 cuttings of several hundreds of varieties, he established nurseries in the Hunter River district about 100 miles north of Sydney.

Wine-making is now one of Australia's primary industries and the annual output runs into many millions of pounds. It is established in the south-east corner of the continent, in New South Wales, Victoria and in South Australia near Adelaide, producing wines of every type and indeed quality from very common red wines (which are dubbed 'plonk' by the natives) to a few carefully made wines, made by individual growers and which, I am afraid, you will have to visit Australia to drink. The bulk of Australian wines are either drunk domestically or exported to England and other countries, and a great deal of it, I fear, is sold to those countries which under-produce for their market, but whose shippers are not averse to mixing it with their own local wine and do not trouble to add the word 'Australian' to the label.

Viticulture in Australia is an extremely serious business and carefully controlled to avoid the introduction of pests from abroad, and a great quantity of perfectly sound wine is produced. It can never, by reason of soil and climate, be termed great or perhaps even fine, but the best of it is very drinkable and is sold at a moderate price. It is in this market that the Australian wine finds its place, with very large quantities of well-made sound wines of a fairly high quality but with no pretensions to greatness, and, rightly enough, the Australian *vigneron* does not trouble to put a date on the neck label of his bottle. The climate is much the same in any year, and, in any case, the wines are made to be drunk young, although they have keeping qualities and travel well in bulk.

In all the states where wine is made, however (that is

the states of Western Australia, Victoria and New South Wales), there are single vineyard wines of tremendous quality and importance. These wines are made essentially for the great State Fairs that are held in Australia and where the ultimate honour is to be awarded a gold medal. Consequently all the best wine growers make up to 1,000 gallons of wine (it is stipulated that the wine shown must not be less than 500 gallons) and this is entered into the competition at the State Fair. I have been privileged to drink many of these gold and silver medal wines, and have been given some to take away (alas! they got no farther than my hotel room) and I can vouch for their outstanding and splendid quality, some of which rubs off on the ordinary wines of the wine grower, which can be bought today in England as well as in Australia.

It is true, I suppose, to say that there is a similarity between certain types of Australian wine and their opposite numbers in Europe, but it is a similarity rather than a family resemblance; it is understandable that in order to market them, the Australian shippers gave the wines the names of the European types rather than call them Murray River or Hunter River, Adelaide and so on; such wines would have been extremely difficult to market and the Australian names would have conveyed nothing to the buyer. On the other hand, there can be no such thing as an Australian Hock or an Australian Chablis, and least of all, an Australian claret or Burgundy, and it might well have been better to give them the names of the grapes, like *Riesling* or *Semillon*, *Cabernet* or *Malbec*, but, however, this is a well-explored argument on both sides, and for good or ill the various types of wine are sold under the names of their European approximations.

Considerable care in the making, storage and bottling of

wine is exercised at both ends – in Australia and in London or wherever the wines are exported to – with the result that the quality is even, and the wine in this country from Australia may be bought with confidence. They are usually quite high in alcoholic content and the wines are well made and pleasant to drink. Like any other class of wine, they should be selected by trial and error from your reputable wine merchant, and I do not think I can add to what I have said already. I could certainly write a lot more about them, but there is no great point in it. The object of this book is to describe the kinds of wine that are available to you, and to encourage you, by trial and error, to drink what you like and like what you drink.

New Zealand wines (writing in 1972) are still a long way behind the best Australian wine, but they are catching up fast. The somewhat colder climate of New Zealand does not make a very sweet wine but they have considerable character, and the vineyards on the North Island are being taken in hand and developed with a great deal of enthusiasm. Mr Frank Thorpy has just published a splendid book of the wines of New Zealand which encourages one to think they have a bright future.

NORTH AMERICA

It is perhaps a pity that we are given no opportunity to taste American wines in this country, for some of them are remarkably good, and while, as in the case of South Africa and Australia, they take unto themselves the name of their European approximation, they have a good deal of character. The main wine-making areas are California and New York State, although a certain amount is made in other parts, but not on the same vast scale. The Californian industry is indeed vast and such is the production that specially built tanker ships bring the wine from California through the Panama Canal and deliver it on the eastern seaboard. These wines are, of course, cheap beverage wines, sold at very low prices, corresponding to the 'plonk' of Australia, although they are often blended with better wines; they have nothing to do with some of the important vintages made in the Napa Valley and similar districts in California. Here may be found some really very fine wines indeed, and although they do not vary much from year to year (the date on the neck label may be and probably is a true date, but is hardly necessary) they are extremely palatable and, even in America, very expensive. The wines do not vary much in quality by year, for the simple reason that the climate does not vary, and the temperature and the sun on the 20th August one year is almost certain to be the same as on the 20th August every other year. This only applies, of course, to California, but in up-state New York there are considerable variations in temperature and a considerable difference in the quality of the wine turned out each year, although the wine-makers tend to correct this by careful blending.

There is a considerable history of the cultivation of the vine in America and it is in fact indigenous. The wild grapes were found by the first of the Conquistadors who came from a solidly wine-drinking country, and it did not take them long to get busy and make themselves some wine, as may be imagined – communications with their mother country, Spain, were, to say the least of it, unreliable. Whatever the quality of the wine, they made it, drank it, and cultivated the grape through the centuries and, of course, imported grafts from the best stocks in Europe in order to improve the quality of the grape. This was not altogether a one-way traffic; the American vines were much more hardy than the French, and in the second half of the nineteenth century a

181

number of experimental stocks were sent from America to France in order to try to improve the native vines. Alas! in the roots of those American stocks was a microscopic bug called the phylloxera and we have already read of what happened when the phylloxera bug jumped from the immune American stock on to the juicy root of the native stock beside it. We now have an odd situation: all the French vineyards, and indeed the vineyards throughout most of Europe, are of American extraction if not actual origin, whereas the majority of the vines grown in America are from French grafts or bred from the original French grafts.

A considerable amount of sparkling wine is made in the United States, mostly in California and a lot in up-state New York. Some of it is made by the best French methods and the best of them are very good indeed. In England and Germany, they would not be permitted to call themselves Champagne, because as we have seen it is held here that only wine made from grapes grown in the Champagne district of France is entitled to be called by that name, but this restriction does not apply in the United States. Wine to beware of is that not made by the *méthode champenoise* but which is made from wine artificially sweetened and impregnated with carbonic acid gas in large tanks, but this kind of wine is equally bad in whatever country it may be found.

Many of the best and greatest of the American wines both in California and New York State are made by Frenchmen who have been brought over from some of the greatest vineyards in France, and they do all that can be done to make their wine as in their native land. They have French vines and expertise, they have ample sun, but they have not the soil; one can't have everything.

SOUTH AMERICA

As may be expected, a very great quantity of wine is made in South America, but little of it has the necessary quality for keeping and export. The only wines obtainable in Britain (to my knowledge) are the excellent Chilean wines, and some Argentine wines, both red and white, which are very good at the moderate prices at which they are sold.

Wine-making in South America is said to have been started by the early Spanish missionaries, and is now made in Argentina, Brazil, Uruguay, Chile, Peru and Bolivia. Argentina is by far the largest producer, with vineyards in more than twelve provinces. Sparkling wines, brandies and vermouths are also made.

10. BOTTLES AND GLASSES

The first wine bottle was not a bottle at all; it was an earthenware jar and it was made to stand upright on an earthen floor. The wine was kept and sealed in it, probably not with a bung, for no corks existed, but with olive oil, and it is still possible in parts of Italy to find in a farmhouse a great Ali Baba kind of jar of wine, with olive oil floating on the top, through which the farmer or his wife will dip a scoop in the centre of the jar to bring out the wine. The wine is thus kept from the air and doesn't go bad or turn to vinegar, whereas if it were not sealed so it would start to go off very soon indeed. These jars were found in Egyptian tombs and in all wine-growing countries, but with the invention of glass came the bottle, and with the invention of the cork came the opportunity of both storing and preserving wine, the importance of which we have noted in the chapter on the Service of Wine (p. 24).

Wine bottles were blown in different shapes in different places and they have grown up traditionally, thus the long Bordeaux bottle with its square shoulders and the sloping Burgundy bottle, and the long narrow Hock or Moselle bottle, and if we exclude the oddities, the standard bottle sizes are something like this:

THE HALF BOTTLE contains 1/12 of a gallon (on an average).

THE IMPERIAL PINT contains, as you will expect, an Imperial pint.

THE BOTTLE, only approximately $\frac{1}{6}$ gallon, as there are various sizes of bottle, some containing 75 centilitres and some wine would be contained in an 80-centilitre bottle, although the actual contents vary by custom, district to district. There are also litre bottles which contain one-third more than the ordinary bottle, but are usually used only for cheap beverage wines throughout Europe; that is the kind of wine sold in a wine shop where one takes an empty bottle to get it replaced with a full one, and the wine is sold by the litre.

Then comes:

THE MAGNUM, which contains two bottles; and then an odd hybrid called by some

THE TRIGNUM which contains three bottles, or in Scotland, it is called a Tappit hen; this is comparatively rarely found and certainly is not in general use.

THE JEROBOAM is a double magnum – that is, it contains four bottles.

THE REHEBOAM contains six or seven bottles, but usually six, and this is a comparatively rare bottle indeed, and even rarer is

THE IMPERIALE which can contain eight or nine bottles, and is usually found only in the château-bottlings of Bordeaux. Most of the great châteaux put up a few *Imperiales* and they are brought out for special occasions; usually, alas! wine-traders dinners and not for you and me, but they can be obtained.

THE METHUSELAH is the great granddaddy of all bottles and is only used for Champagne and contains eight or more bottles, but it is something of a fake because the Champagne makers do not bottle the wine as such, but decant wine into the Methuselah for very special occasions from smaller bottles, and recork it. I have never yet seen a Methuselah in action, but André Simon tells me that it is served by the wine waiter who holds the neck of the bottle in his right hand, with his enormous container tucked under his arm.

185

Some bottles are extremely beautiful, especially the older ones made of handblown glass with variations in type and size and sometimes with shoulder seals moulded on to the shoulder of the bottle, which may have a coat of arms, or the name of a château, or in the case of port, the shipper and the date, and sometimes the initials of a private person or college or club lucky enough to be able to buy bottles in sufficient quantity. Some châteaux will celebrate a very special vintage by putting up their château bottles with a shoulder seal of this kind. Lafite did in 1945, for instance. The enterprising people who devised the bottle for the alleged Napoleon Brandy (whoever they may be) emphasized that it was in fact Napoleon Brandy by putting a shoulder seal on the bottles with a very beautiful 'N' moulded on it. Could any further proof be necessary that it came from the cellars of the Emperor himself?

It is perfectly true that the bigger the bottle the better the wine, but only in this sense: that since all impurities must get into the wine through the cork, there is chance of fewer impurities entering through one cork than through four, in the case of the Jeroboam, and certainly I have drunk some very splendid wines from big bottles. On the other hand, it can be pretty disastrous to find a corked Jeroboam of Champagne which must be consigned to the sink.

Just as the first 'bottle' was a jar, so the first 'glass' was a cup, and it was not until clear glass became available that the full pleasure of drinking a lovely wine could be enjoyed to the full. It has been well said that in enjoying our wine, we indulge four out of five senses, taste of course, and smell, hearing (for is not the popping of the cork a nice thing to hear?) and not least of these, sight. The contemplation of a glass of red wine in a clear glass against a candle is an

Bottles and Glasses

These are the shapes that I would recommend to you and which can be bought quite cheaply from most good stores:

1. *Sherry:* 2. *Port:* 3. *Claret or Burgundy:* 4. *Champagne – modern*

5. *Champagne – flute:* 6. *Hock, Moselle or Alsace:* 7. *Old type Hock or Moselle:* 8. *Brandy*

187

extremely pleasant matter, and if the glass be beautiful and rounded and nicely made, we can perhaps indulge the sense of touch too. A sixth sense may also come into action, that of anticipation, but this is nothing to do with glasses. For hundreds of years, glasses have been made in many shapes and sizes; they have been beautifully engraved and sometimes, very wrongly in my opinion, they are made of coloured glass. Those glasses which have been designed by modern designers for wine-lovers are nearly all tulip-shaped, large or small according to the wine which is used, and made of clear crystal with little or no cutting, so that the sight of the wine is unimpaired.

Champagne can be enjoyed out of flute glasses – that is to say, long, thin needle-shaped glasses from whence the bubbles rise interminably for the whole time the wine is in the glass, which is not usually all that long. The use of the modern wedding reception flat bowled type of Champagne glass is to be deplored – the wine explodes in it and effervesces and goes flat very quickly and does the wine no justice, and you will not find these glasses in general use outside England or America. Brandy glasses should be *ballon* shaped, but small enough to hold in the palm of the hand so that the wine may be warmed.

Good clear wine glasses are not necessarily expensive, and indeed they should be cheap because they should be in general use and breakages are, unfortunately, all too frequent. I suppose the general principle is to pay as much as one can afford and even the plainest glasses by Baccarat, the famous French glass manufacturers, are extremely expensive by any standard, but they are lovely things and if I were a rich man, I should certainly use them all the time. As it is, I use a perfectly simple plain (Czechoslovakian I suspect), goblet, which I can buy in all sizes, which does full credit to the wine inside it. The use of large glasses, *grandes pièces* they are sometimes called, in fashionable restaurants, is harmless enough and, of course, tends to use up a bottle very much more quickly (which I suppose is the general idea), besides the conceit. It is, I confess, rather a pleasant conceit and one restaurant that I have in mind only uses it for the very best Burgundies at very high prices which enables the host to show his guests and the other people in the restaurant that he is buying the most expensive wine.

GLOSSARY

ALEATICO: A black muscat grape, grown in parts of Italy, and the name given to wine made therefrom.

APPELLATION CONTRÔLÉE: Standards laid down regulating geographical limitations, minimum alcoholic strength and other conditions which must be satisfied before a wine may be sold as *Appellation Contrôlée*.

ARINTO: A white grape grown in Portugal, from which Bucellas are made.

AUSLESE: German for *selected*, referring to specially chosen grapes.

BARRIQUE: French equivalent of hogshead, which usually contains 50 gallons.

BEERENAUSLESE: German for *selected berries*, chosen after the *auslese*.

BODEGA: Spanish for *cellar* or *wine store*.

CABERNET: Family name for varieties of black grapes grown all over the world.

CHAI: A place for wine storage above the ground.

CHAPTALIZATION: The addition of sugar to the grapes during crushing to increase the degree of alcohol produced.

CHÂTEAU: The homestead of a wine-producing estate, not necessarily a castle.

CHÂTEAU BOTTLED: Wine bottled where it was made, which fact is recorded on the label.

CLARET: Name given to the red wines of Bordeaux.

CLOS: This prefix denotes that the vineyard was once enclosed by a wall or fence.

190

CRU: A vineyard or range of vineyards producing wines of the same quality and standard.

CRUST: A sediment shed by red wines in the bottle.

CUVÉE: French for *vatting*, or blend of wines.

DÉGORGEMENT: Removal of sediment from bottles of Champagne by drawing the first cork after freezing the neck of the bottle to ensure little loss of wine and gas.

DÉGUSTATION: Tasting.

ÉTAMPÉ: French for *branded*, or *stamped* (on the cork).

FORMINT: Quality white grape from which Tokay is made.

FUDER: Moselle wine cask containing about 211 gallons.

GEWURTZTRAMINER: A white grape, grown in Alsace, Austria and Germany.

GRENACHE: A grape grown mainly in the Roussillon area of France, and the name given to the wine produced from these grapes.

LIQUEUR DE L'EXPEDITION: Sweet syrup used for sweetening Champagne when first bottled.

LIQUEUR DE TIRAGE: Sweet syrup used for sweetening Champagne at the time of *dégorgement* (q.v.).

MALVASIA: A species of white grape and the wine made therefrom.

MARC: A spirit distilled from the husks of grapes after the wine has been made.

MUSCAT: Generic name for highly scented varieties of *Vitis vinifera*, grown in Europe and California particularly. Wines made from these grapes are known as *Moscatel* (in Spain), *Moscatello* and *Moscato* (in Italy).

NATUR, NATURREIN: German words indicating the wine has not been sweetened.

PALUS: Low-lying vineyards of the Gironde, producing cheaper types of Claret.

PEDRO XIMENEZ: A particularly sweet grape grown in Spain, and the wine made therefrom.

PHYLLOXERA: *Phylloxera vastatrix*, the American vine louse, which attacks vines.

PINOT: Variety of grape, black and white, from which the best Champagne and the best Burgundies are made.

QUINTA: Portuguese estates upon which vines are grown.

RIESLING: Fine white grapes grown in Alsace, Austria, Germany and Hungary, making high-class white wines.

SAUVIGNON: Species of white grape used for making the best Sauternes and other fine white wines.

SCHLOSS: German for *castle*, or *estate*.

SEKT: German sparkling wine.

SEMILLON: A species of white grape used for making fine white wines.

SOLERA: System of blending sherry from vats laid down in various years.

SPAETLESE: German for *late vintaged* – the wine is made from the last grapes picked in a good year.

STÜCK: The German tun or wine barrel containing usually 300 litres. It can be as large as 600 or 1,200 litres (66, 120 or 240 gallons).

SYLVANER: A white wine grape grown extensively in Germany and in Alsace.

SYRAH: A black grape, chiefly grown in the Rhône Valley for making good red table wines.

TÊTE DE CUVÉE: First drawing-off of the wine from selected over-ripe grapes in the Sauternes district. Best wines from any particular vineyard in Burgundy.

TRAMINER: A white grape grown mainly in Alsace and Germany for the making of high-class wines.

Glossary

TROCKENBEERENAUSLESE: Name given to German wine made from specially selected over-ripe grapes; it is very fine, rich and sweet.

VENDANGE: The vintage or grape harvest.

VERNACCIA: A grape grown in Italy and Sardinia for making red wine.

VIGNERON: Vine-grower.

WACHSTUM: German for 'the property of'; found on German wine labels.

BIBLIOGRAPHY

H. Warner Allen: *A History of Wine* (Faber, 1961)

—— *White Wines and Cognac* (Constable, 1952)

J. M. Broadbent: *Wine Tasting* (Wine & Spirits Publications, 1968)

L. B. Escritt: *The Small Cellar* (Jenkins, 1960)

Patrick Forbes: *Champagne* (Gollancz, 1970)

R. E. H. Gunyon: *The Wines of Central and South-Eastern Europe* (Duckworth, 1971)

S. F. Hallgarten: *Alsace and Its Wine Gardens* (Deutsch, 1957)

—— *Rhineland Wineland* (Elek, 1955)

——(with André L. Simon) *Wines of Germany* (McGraw-Hill, 1963)

Peter Hunt (ed): *Eating and Drinking* (Ebury Press, 1962)

Julian Jeffs: *Sherry* (Faber, 1961)

—— *The Wines of Europe* (Faber, 1961)

Hugh Johnson: *The World Atlas of Wine* (Mitchell Beazley, 1971)

—— *Wine* (Nelson, 1966; Penguin)

A. Langenbach: *German Wines and Vines* (Vista Books, 1962)

T. A. Layton: *Wine Craft* (Harper & Co., 1958)

Alexis Lichine: *Wines of France* (Cassell, 1955)

O. W. Loeb and Terence Prittie: *Moselle* (Faber, 1972)

Edmund Penning-Rowsell: *The Wines of Bordeaux* (David & Charles, 1969)

Raymond Postgate: *The Plain Man's Guide to Wine* (Michael Joseph, 1961)

Bibliography

Raymond Postgate: *Portuguese Wine* (Dent, 1969)

George Rainbird: *Sherry and the Wines of Spain* (Michael Joseph, 1966)

Cyril Ray: *The Wines of Italy* (McGraw-Hill, 1966; Penguin)

J. R. Roger: *The Wine of Bordeaux* (Deutsch, 1960)

P. Morton Shand: *A Book of French Wine* (Cape, 1960; Penguin)

—— *A Book of Wine* (Guy Chapman, 1926)

Alan Sichel: *The Penguin Book of Wines* (Penguin, 1965)

André L. Simon: *English Fare and French Wine* (Newman Neame)

—— *History of Champagne* (Ebury Press, 1962)

—— *Know Your Wines* (Newman Neame, 1956)

—— *The Noble Grapes and Great Wines of France* (McGraw-Hill, 1957)

—— *A Wine Primer* (Michael Joseph, 1946; Penguin)

—— (with S. F. Hallgarten): *Wines of Germany* (McGraw-Hill, 1963)

—— (ed): *Wines of the World* (McGraw-Hill, 1967)

H. W. Yoxall: *The Enjoyment of Wine* (Michael Joseph, 1972)

—— *The Wines of Burgundy* (David & Charles, 1968)

INDEX

Index

Index

Index

Index